Dtp
and
graphic design

Iacob Adrian

Famous Paintings

STUDY

vol. 1

Iacob Adrian

ISBN-13: 978-1479125869
ISBN-10: 1479125865

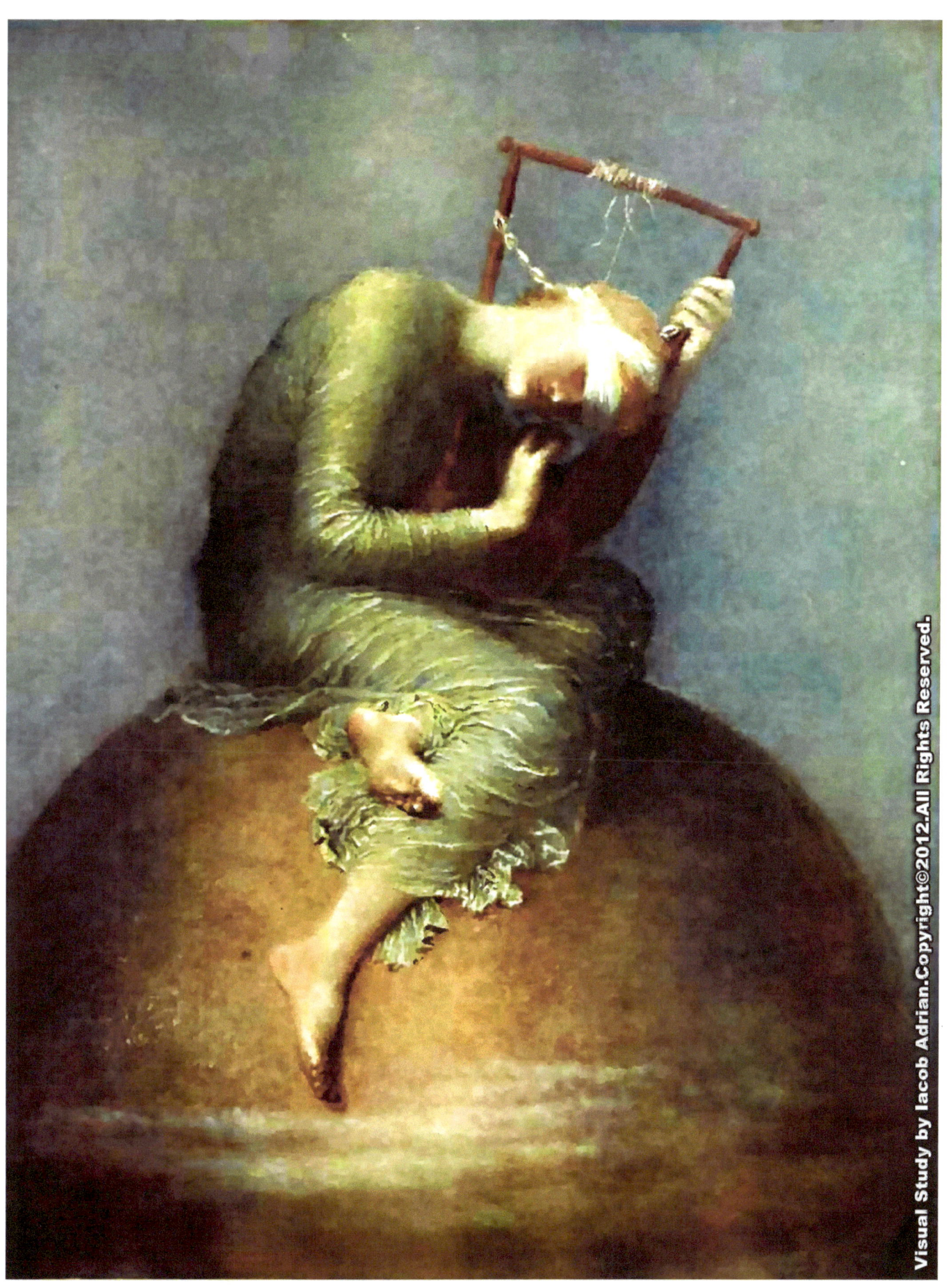

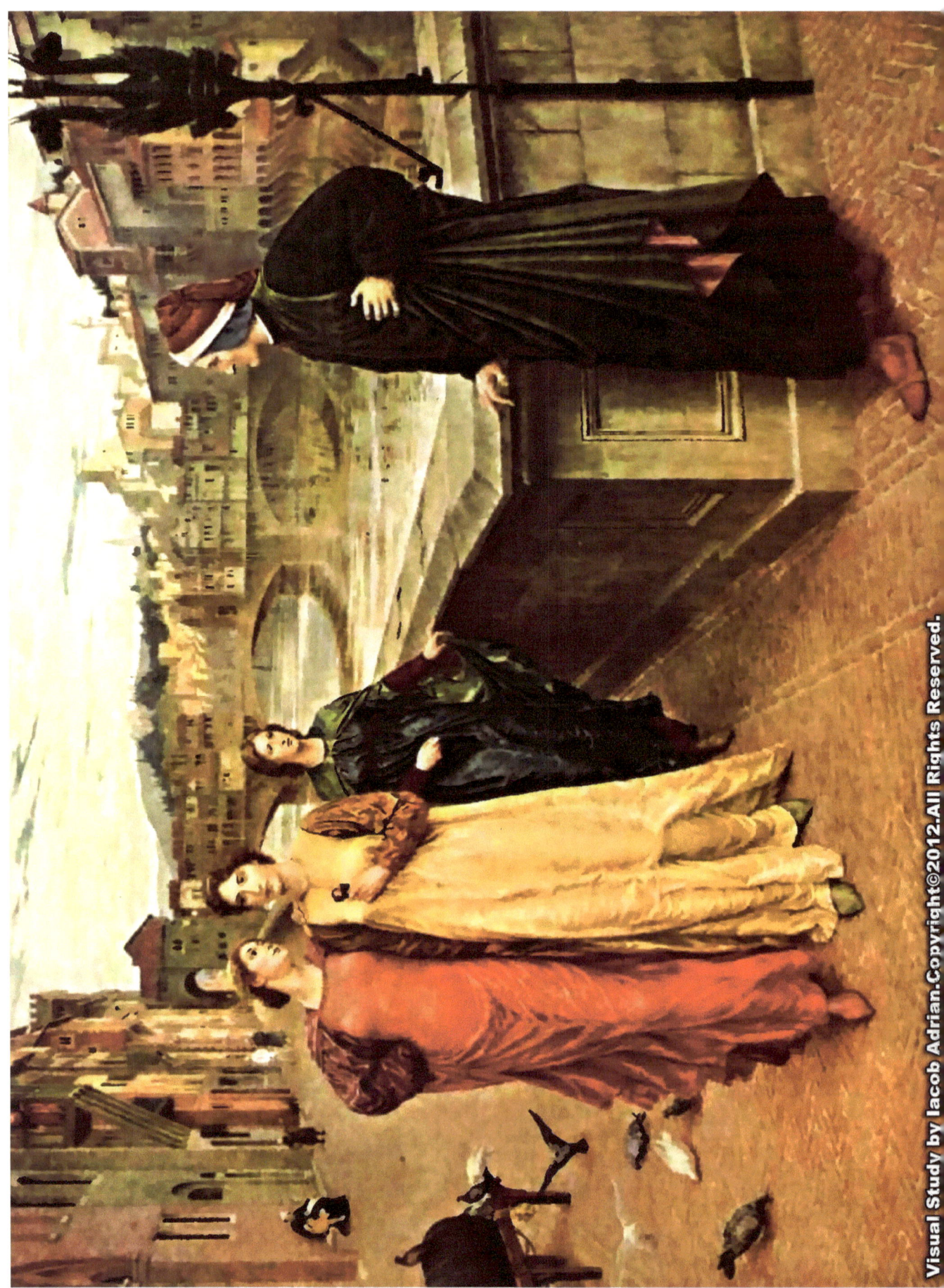

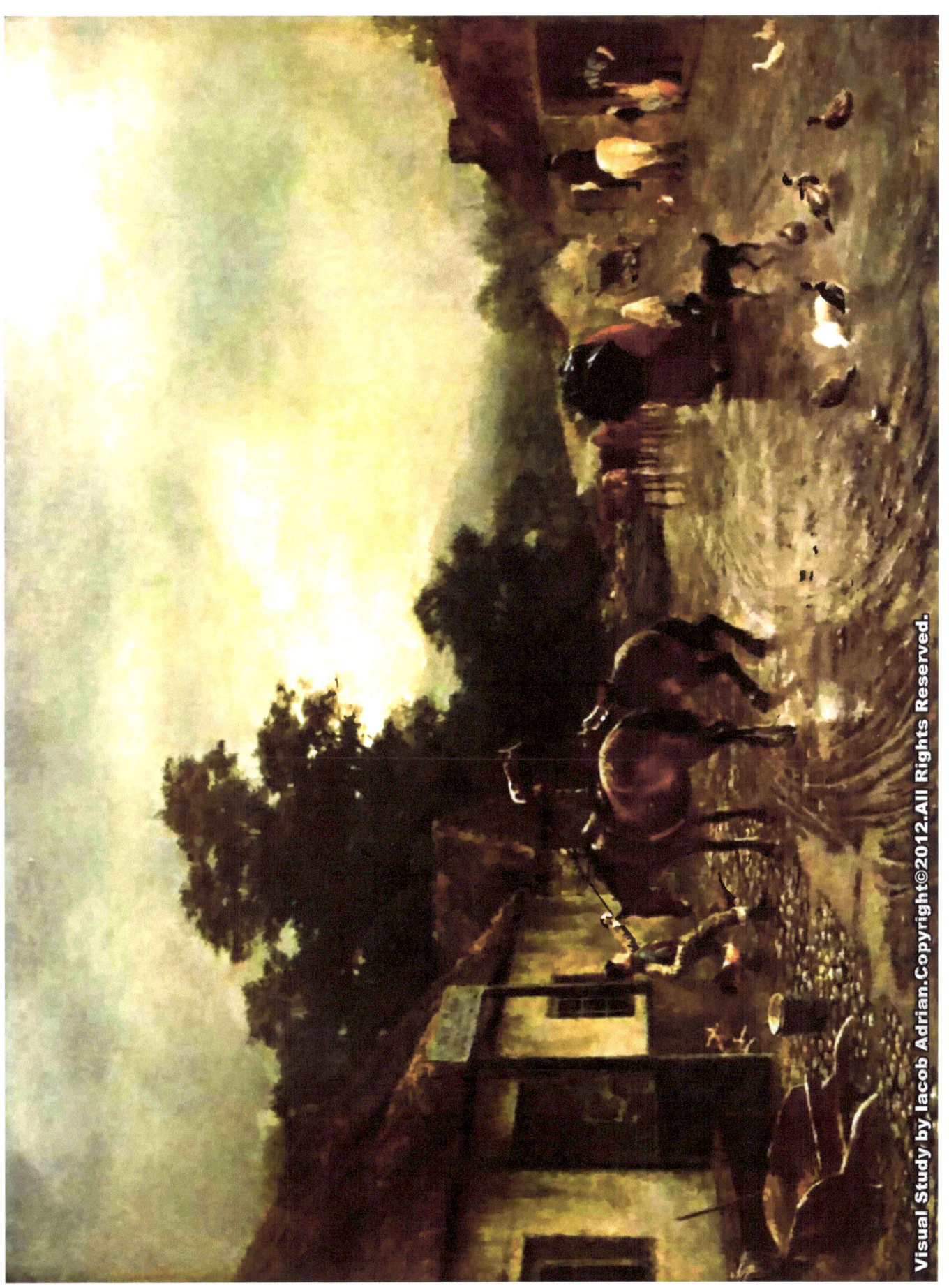

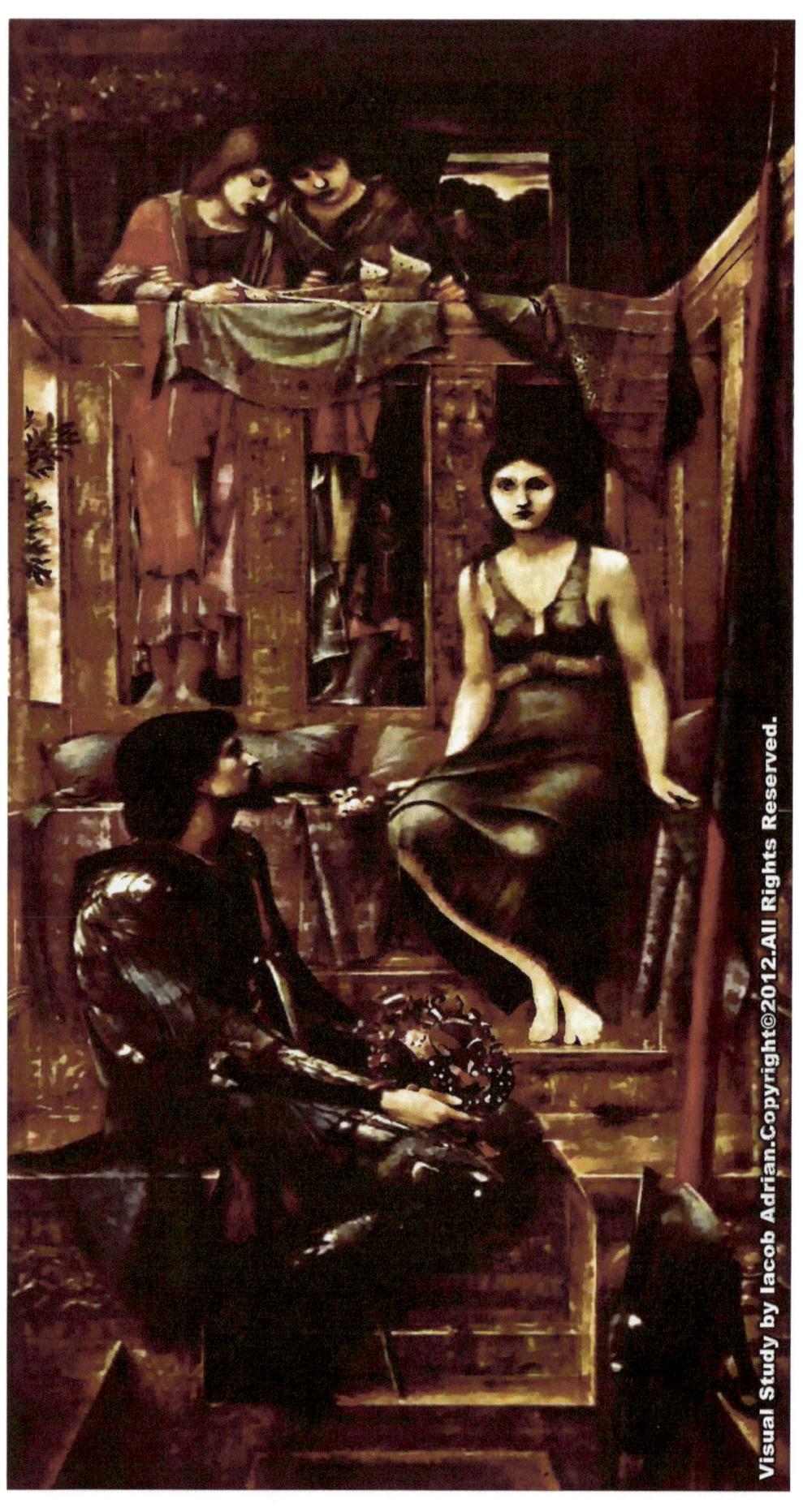

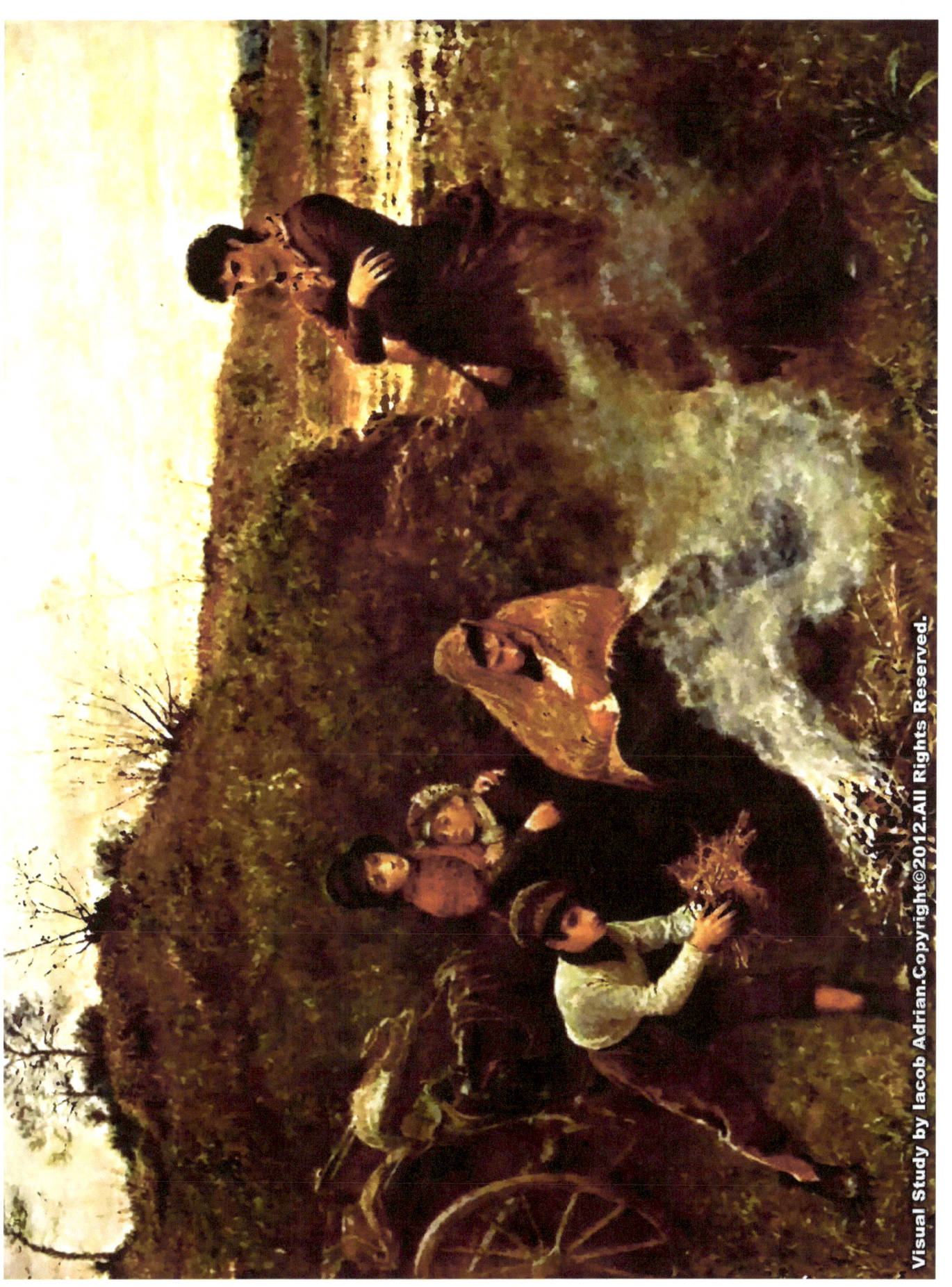

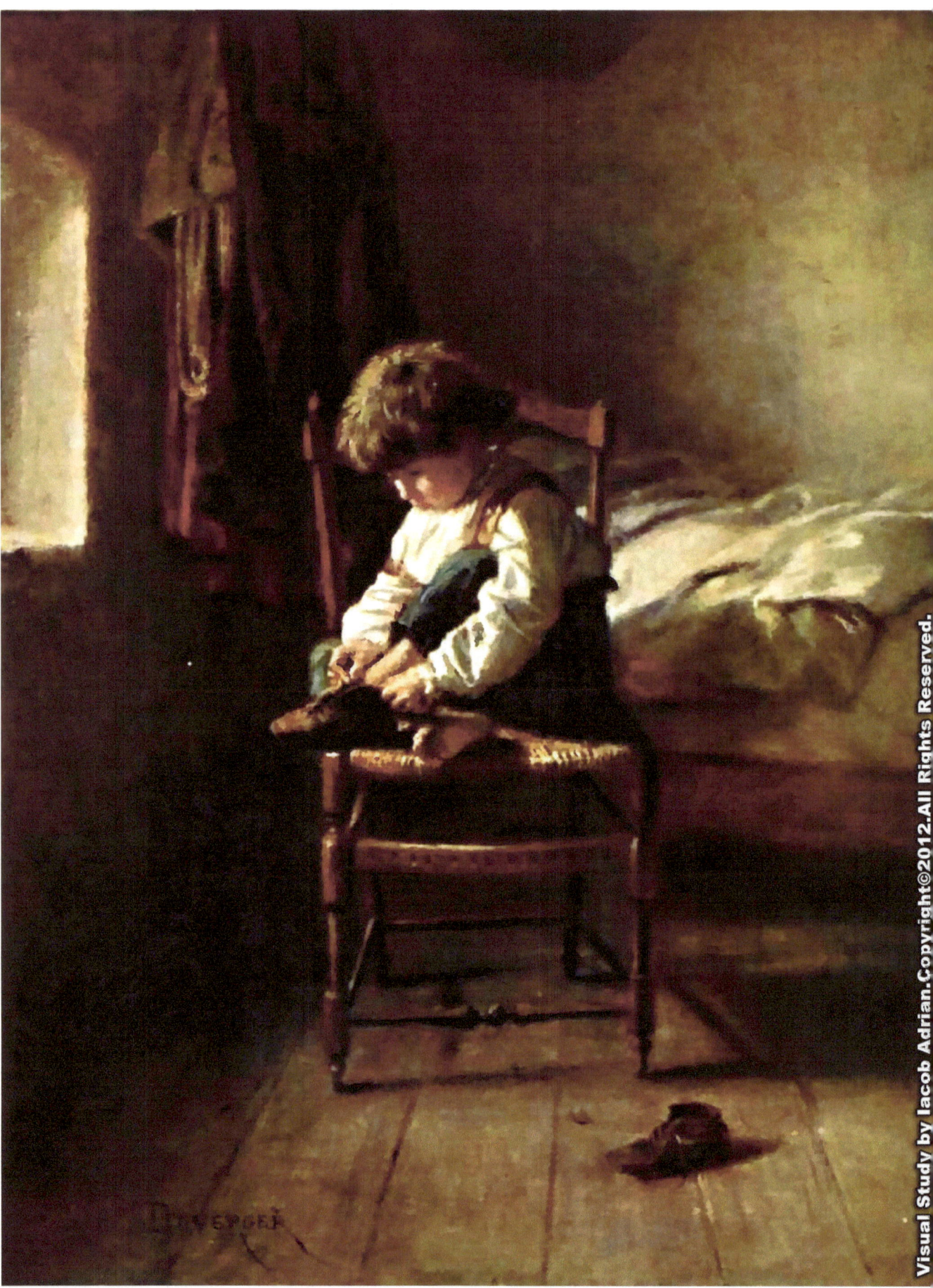

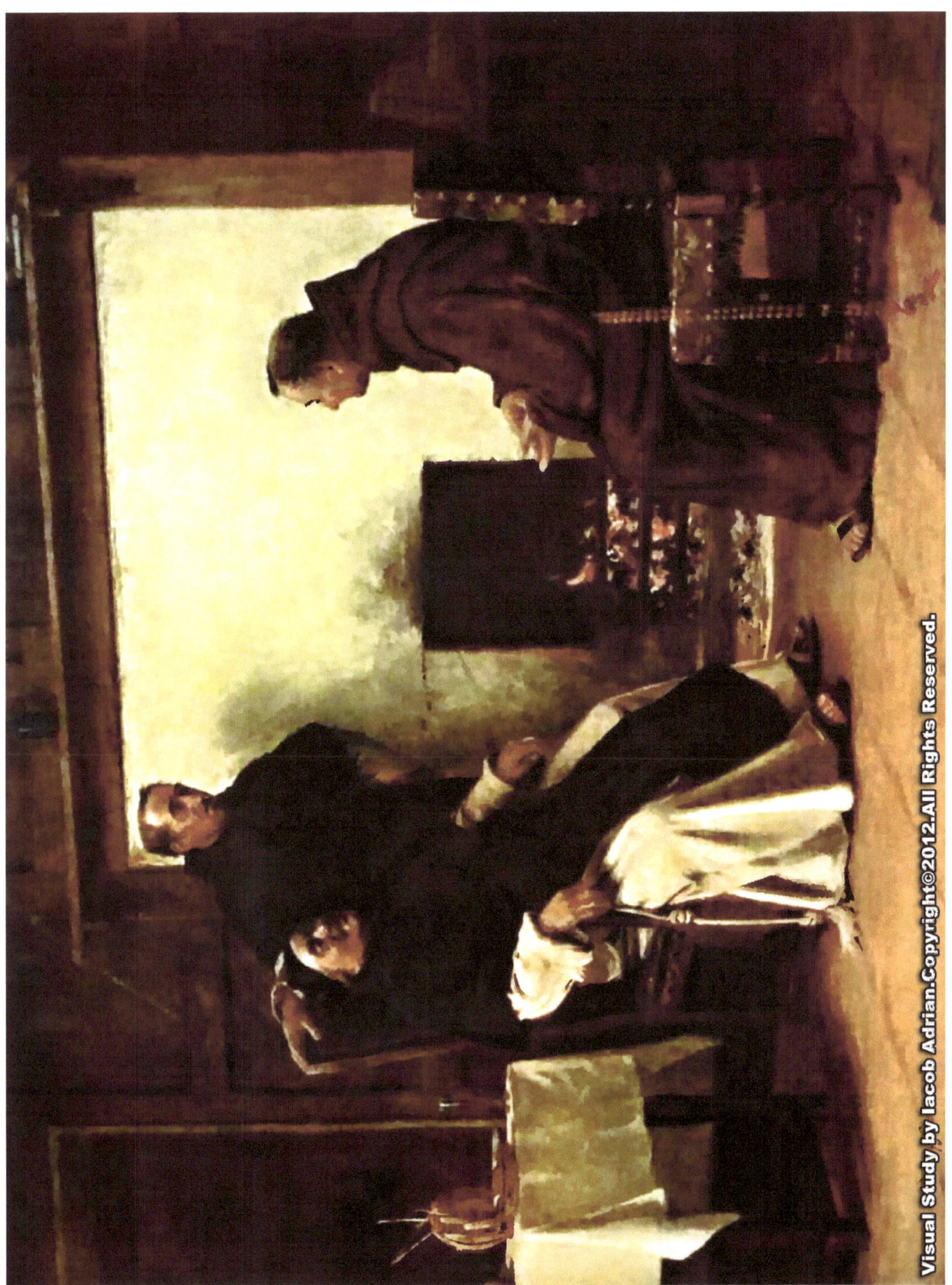

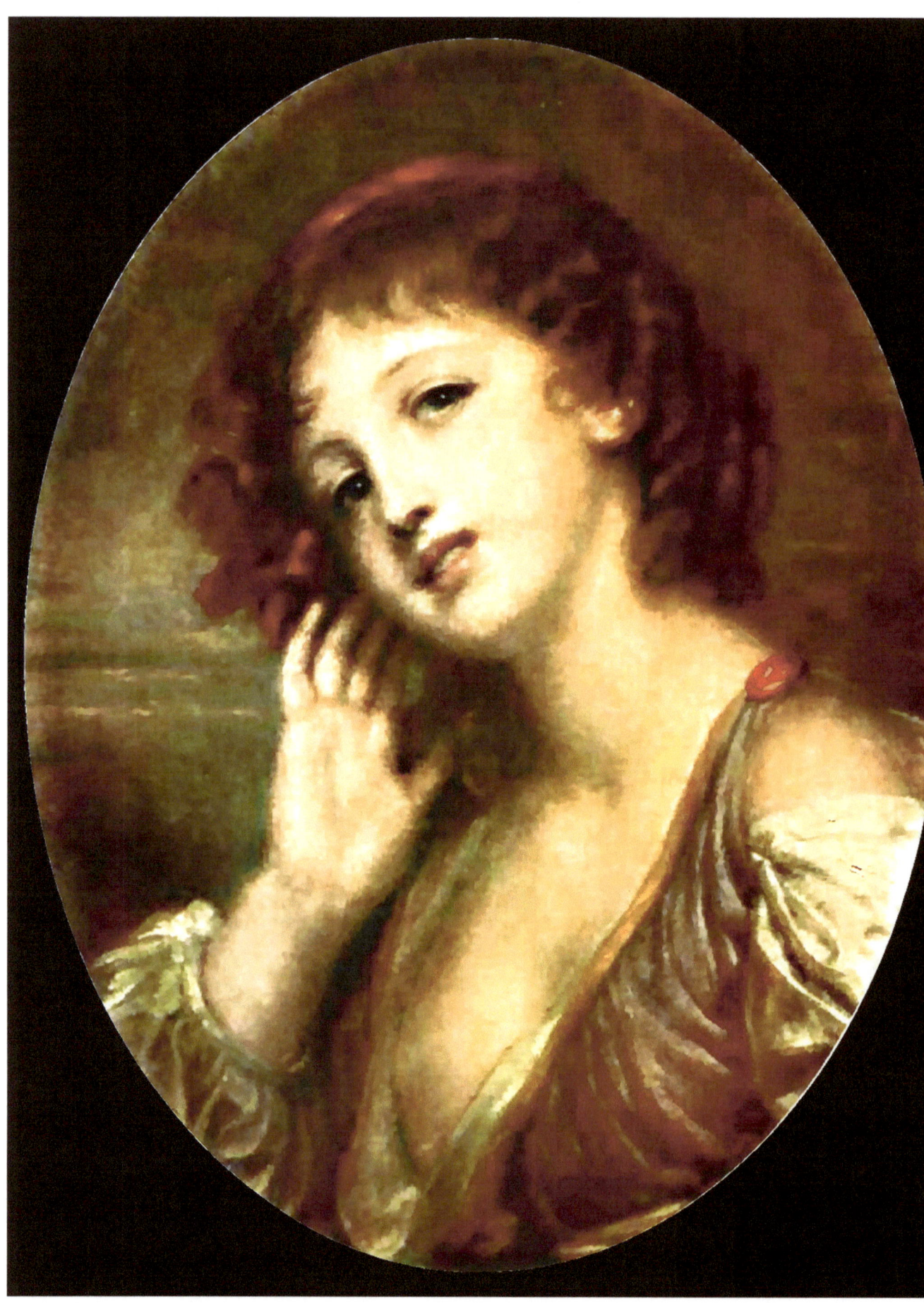

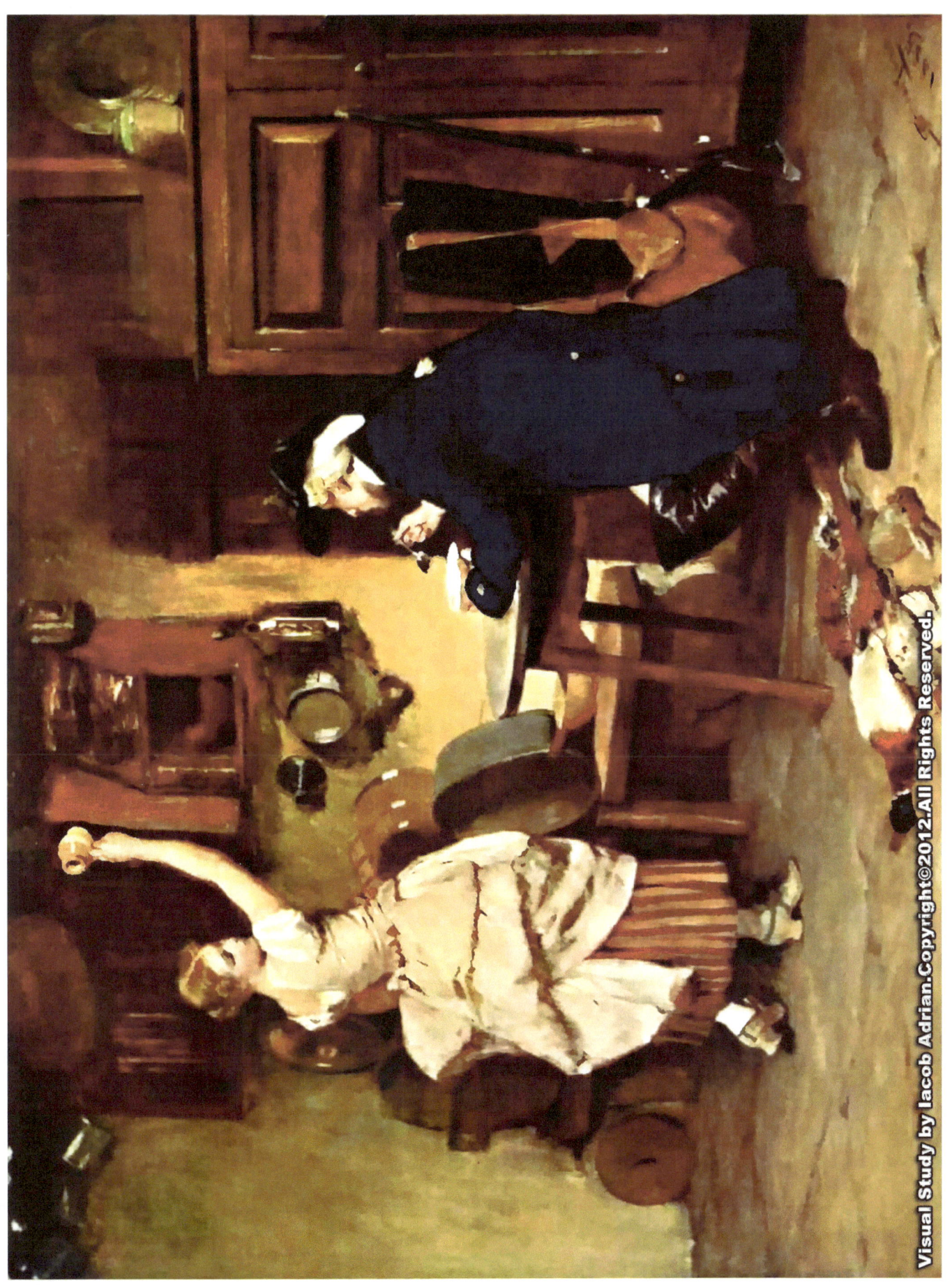

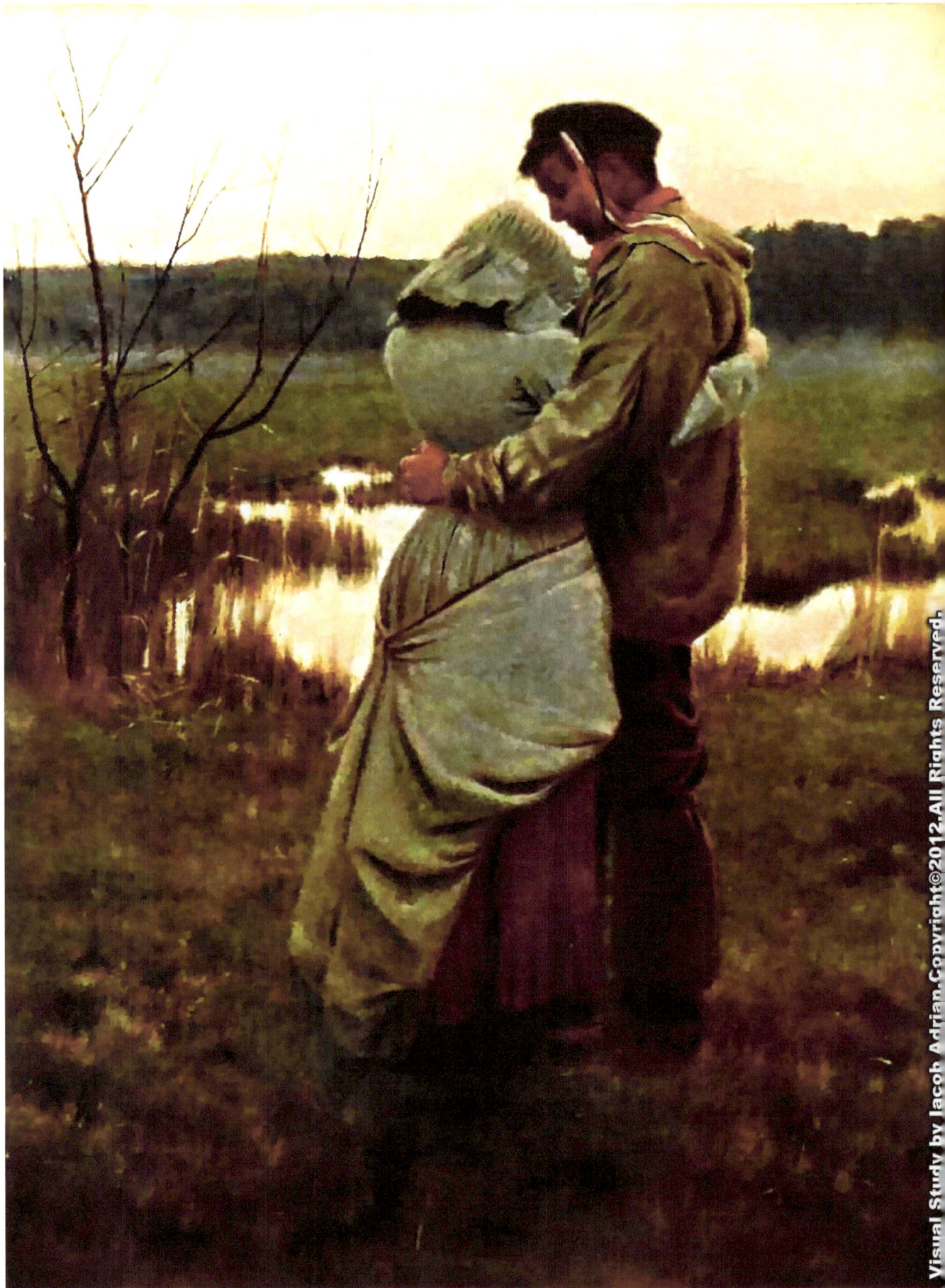

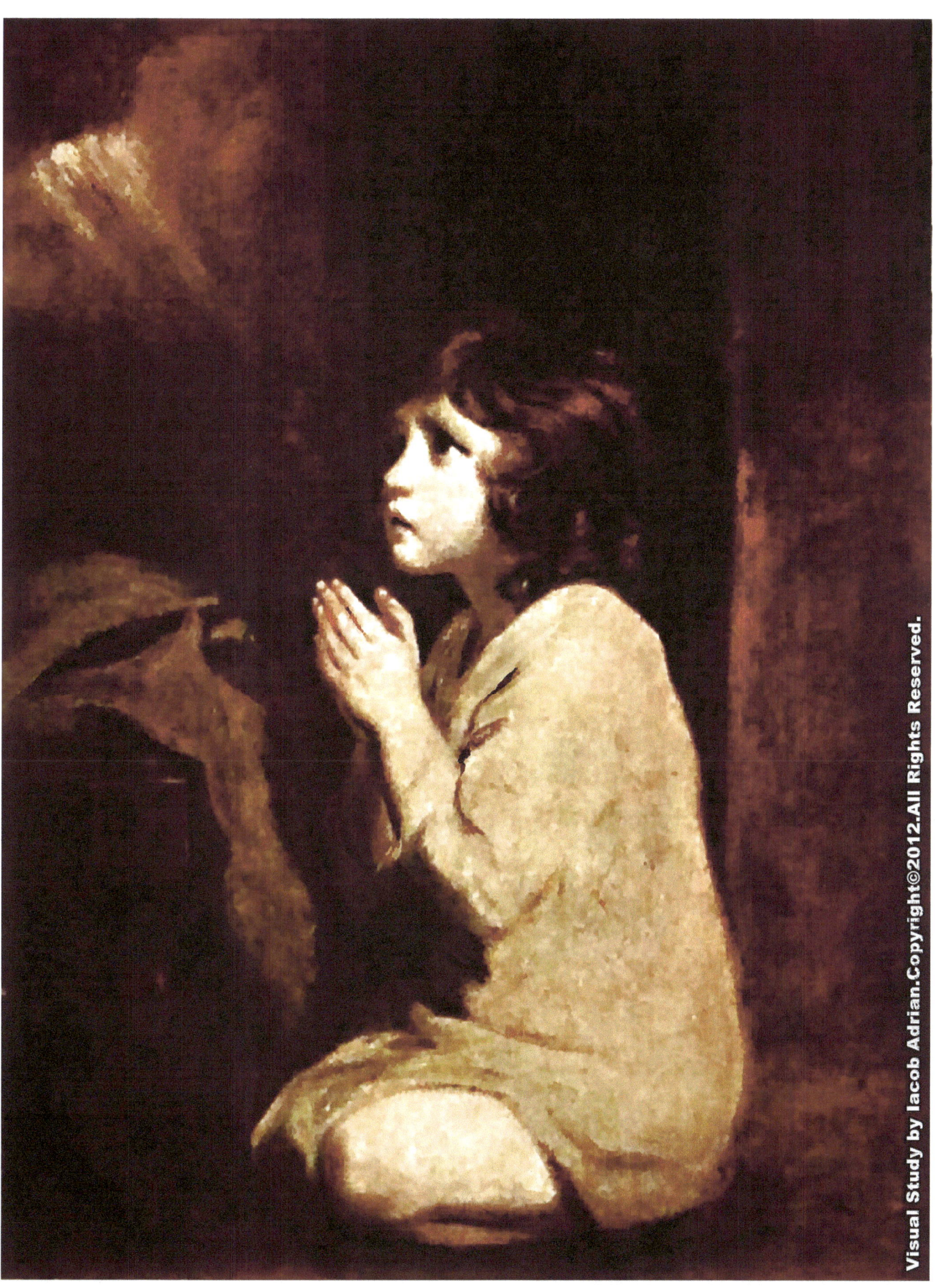

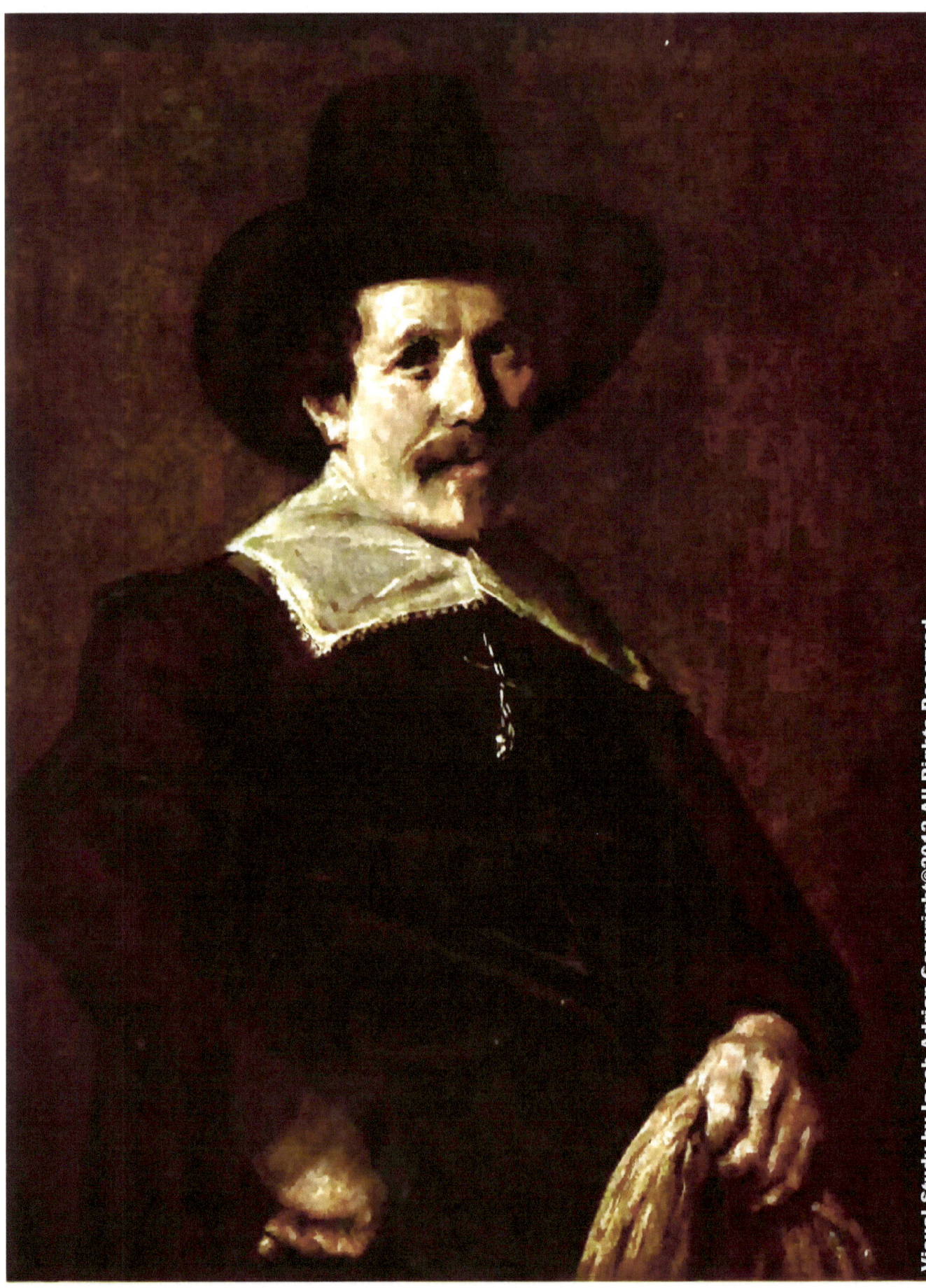

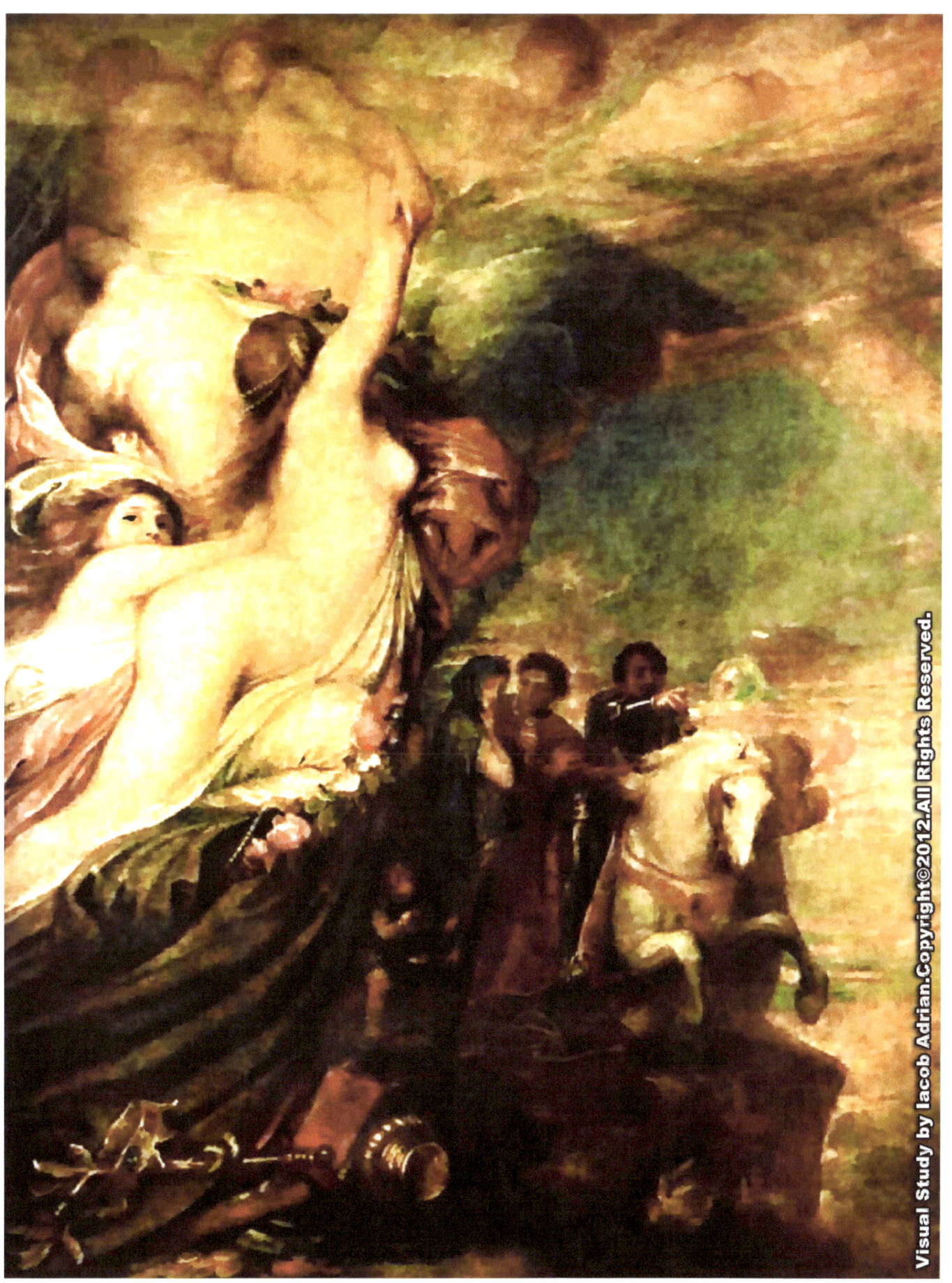

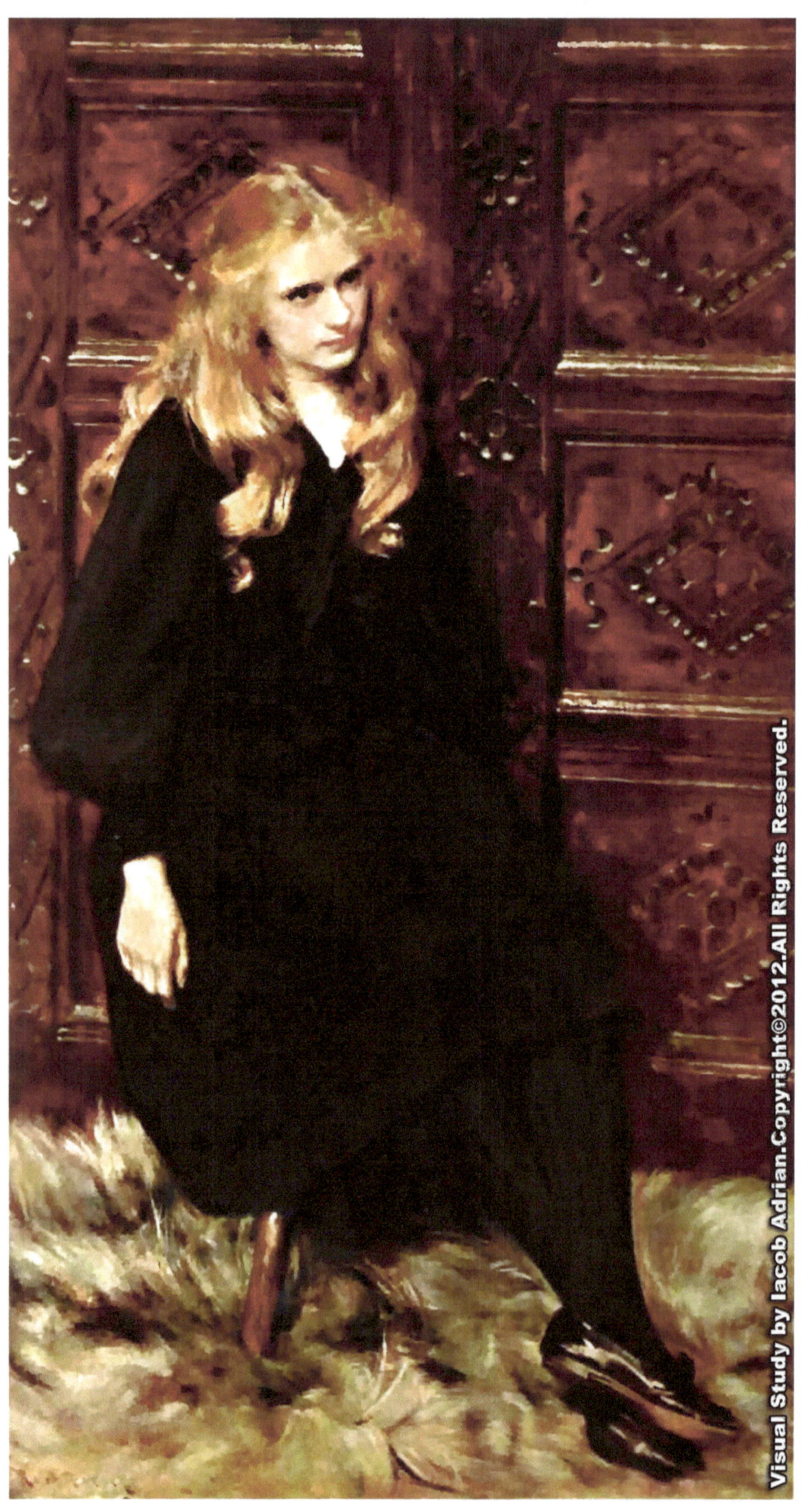

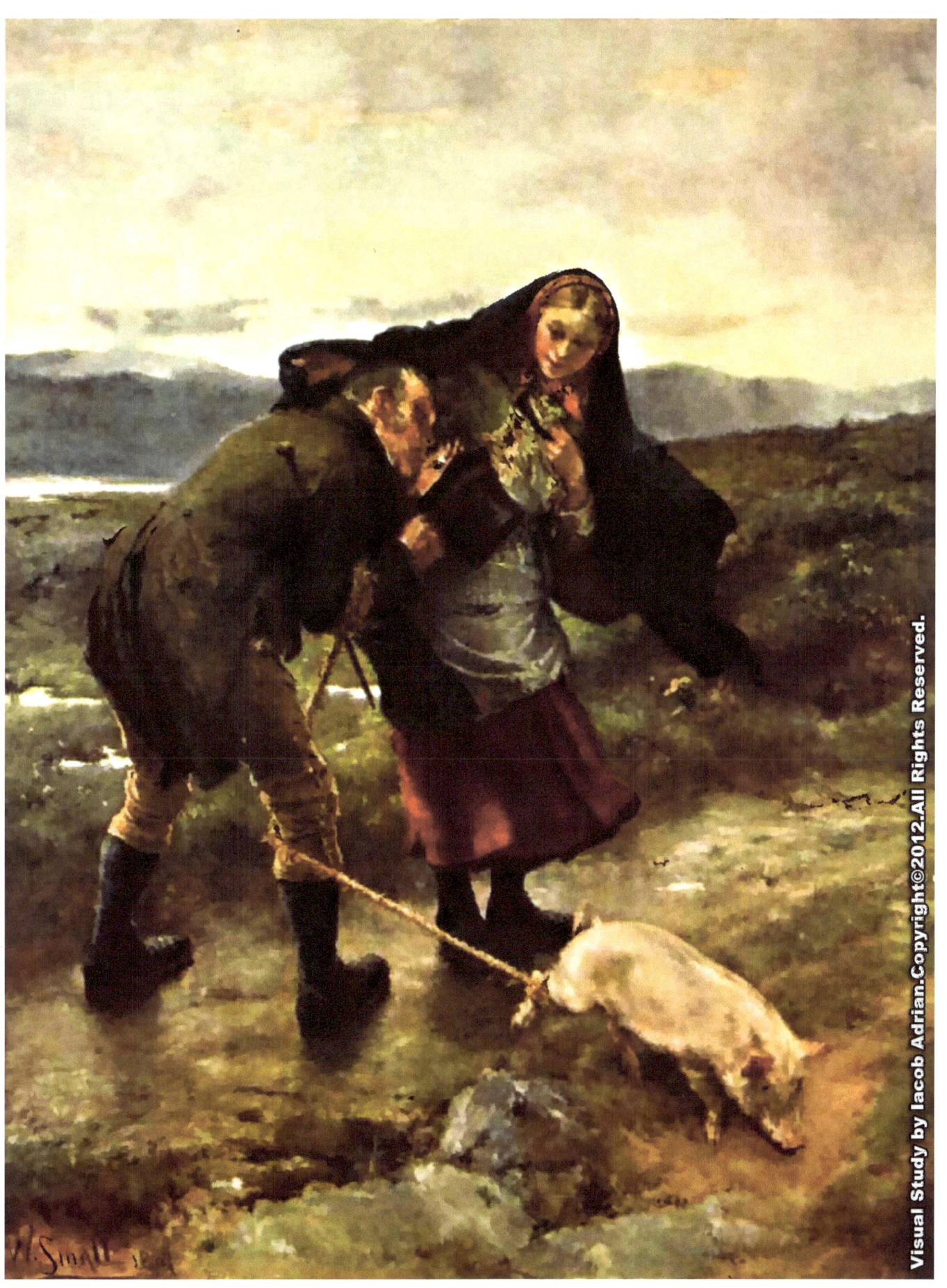

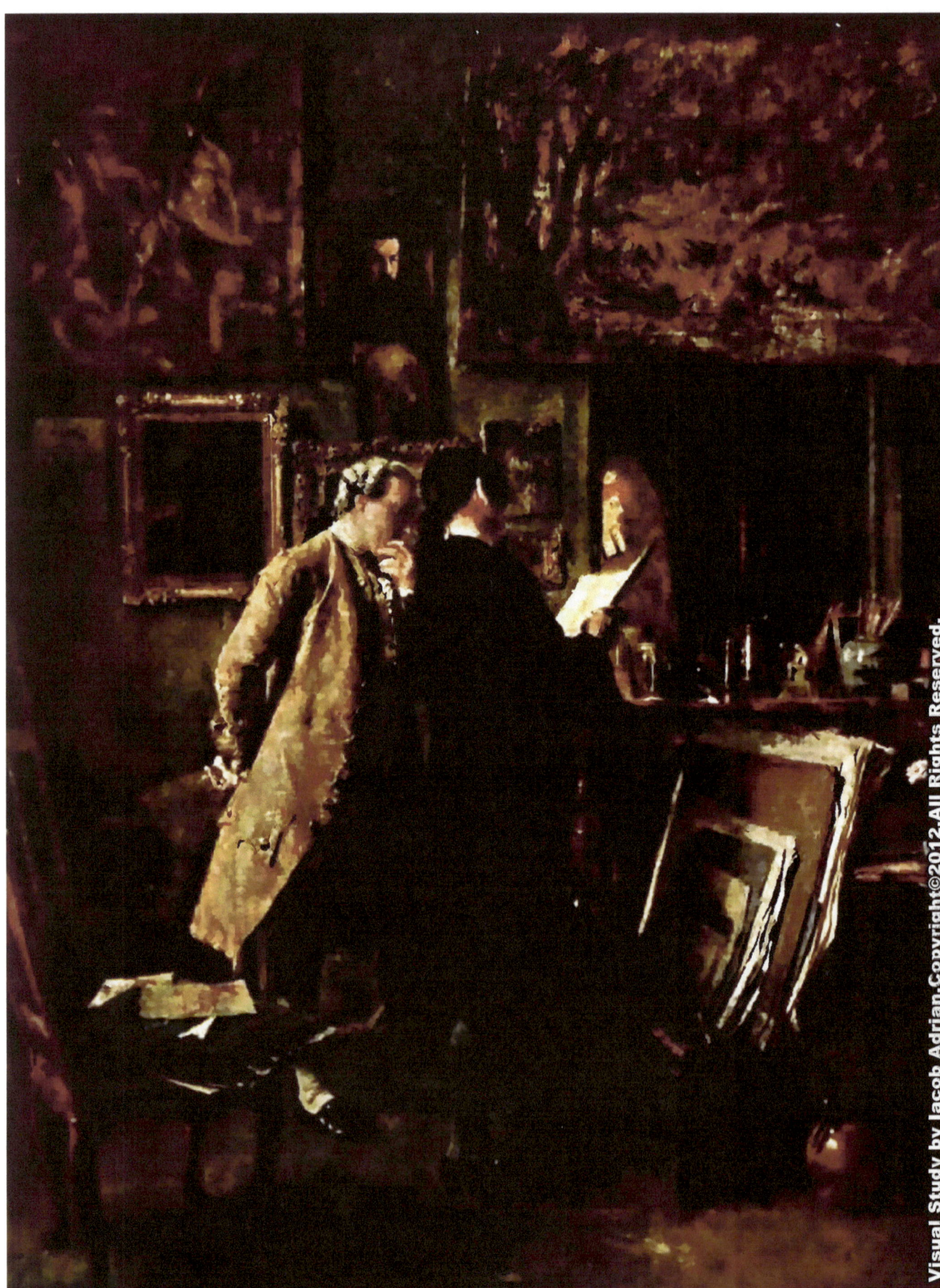

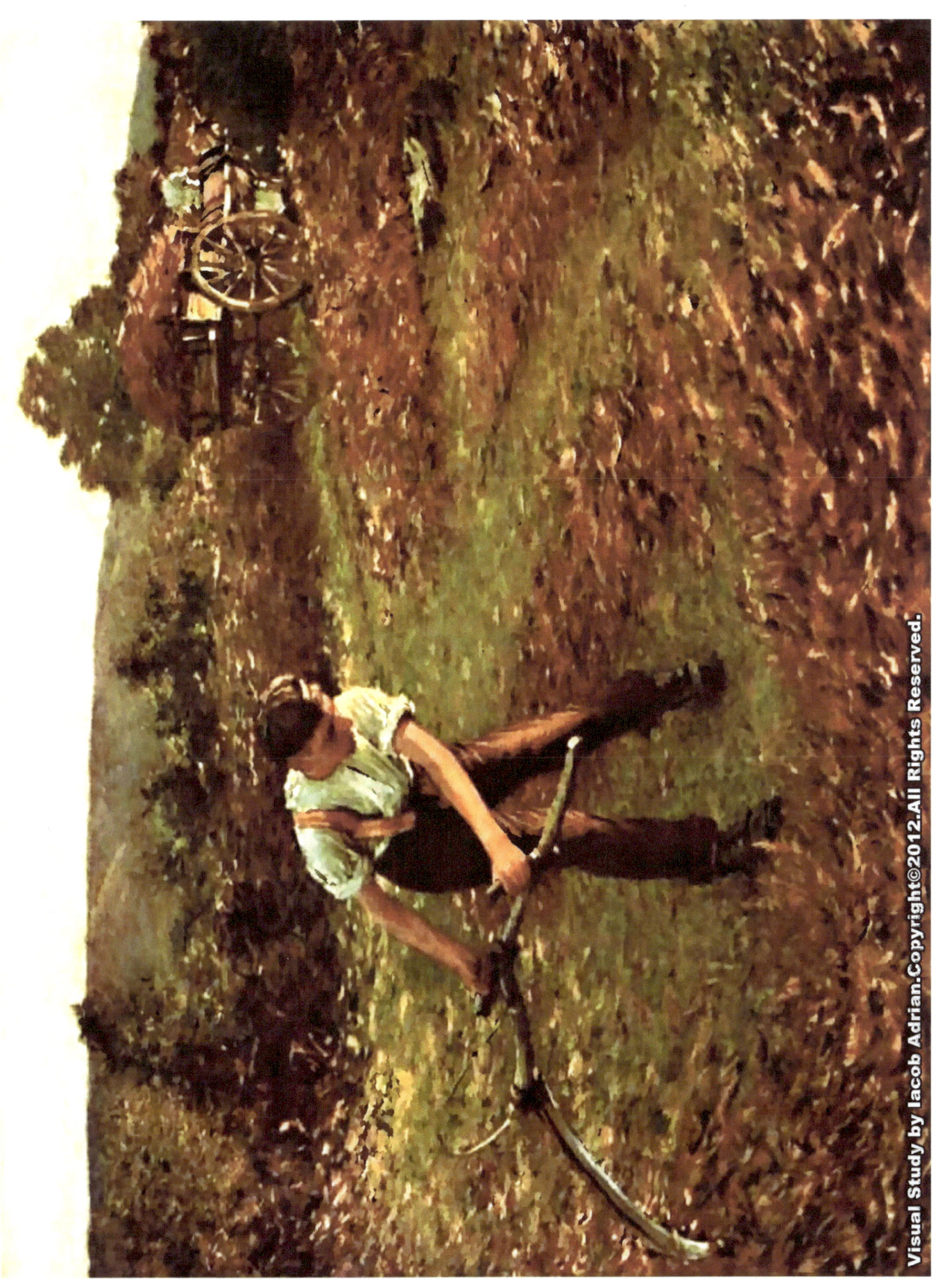

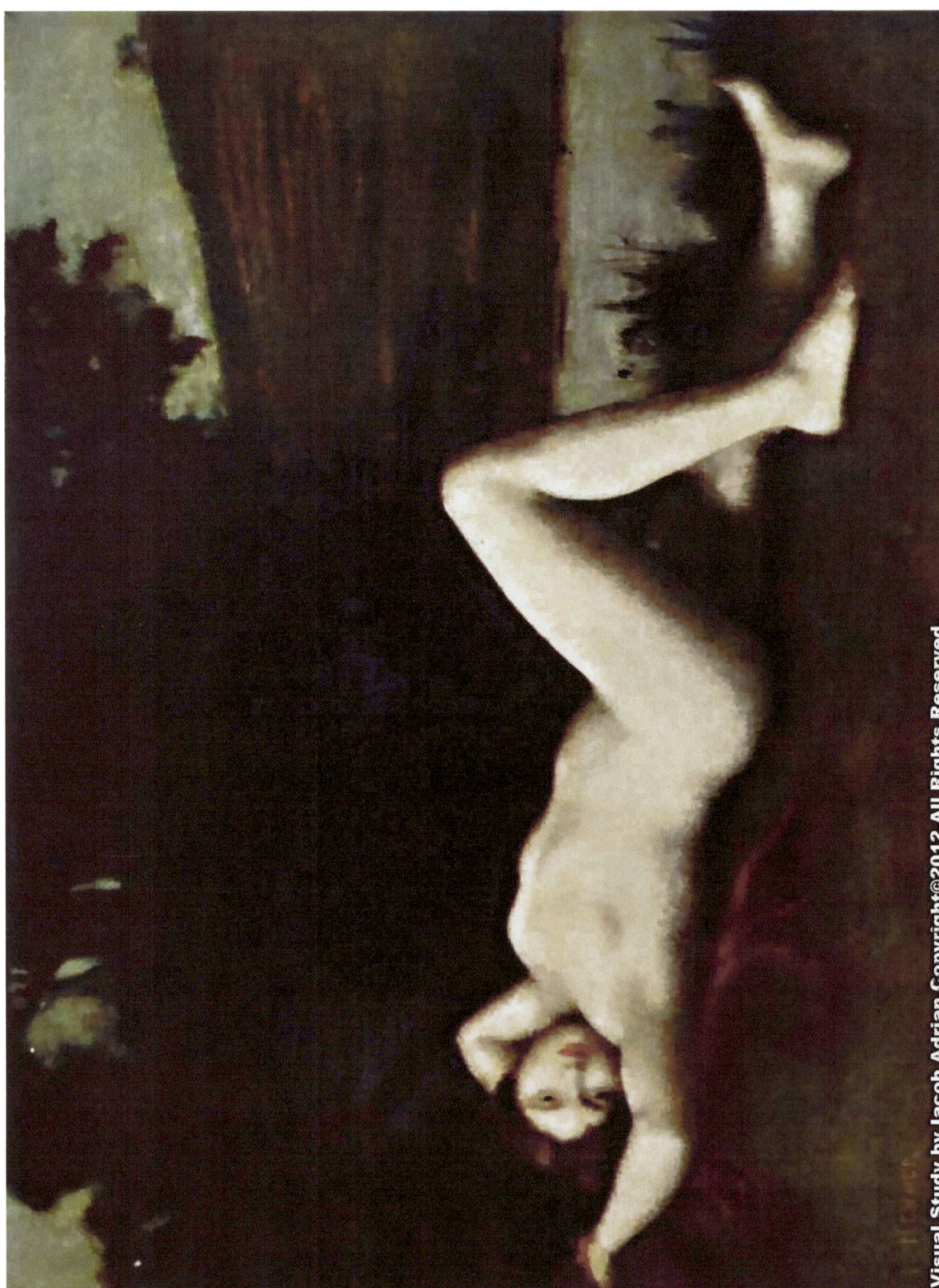

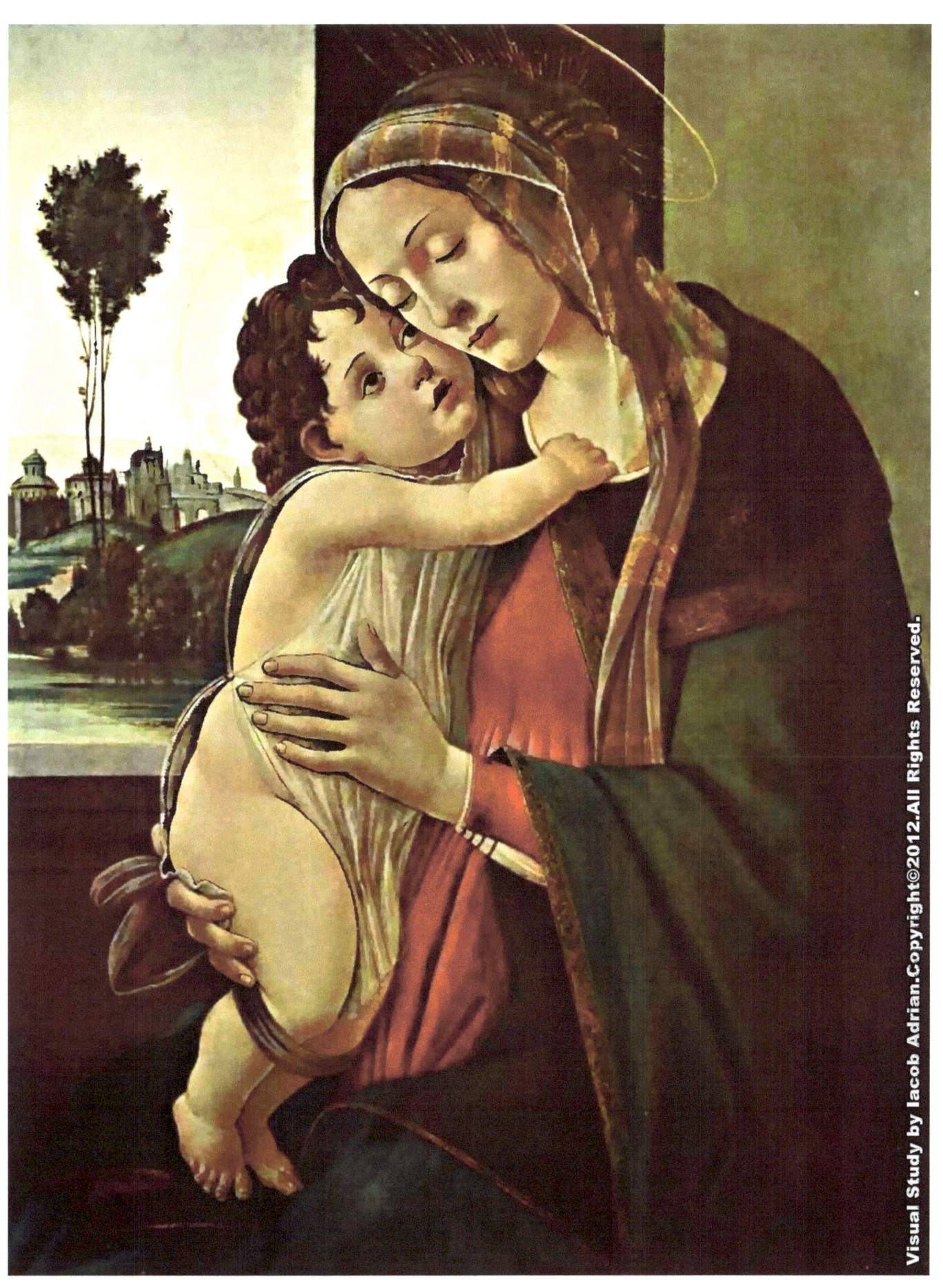

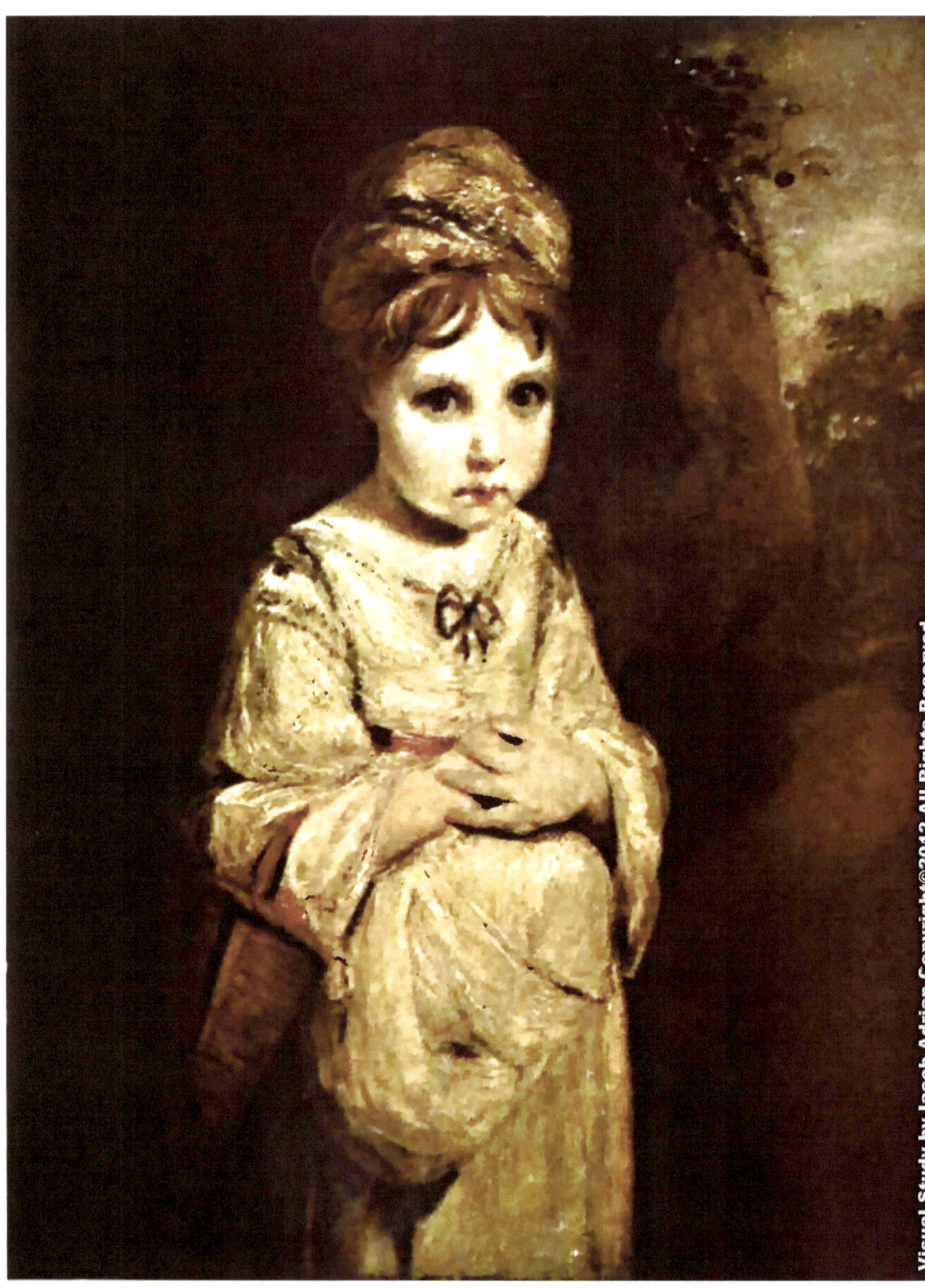

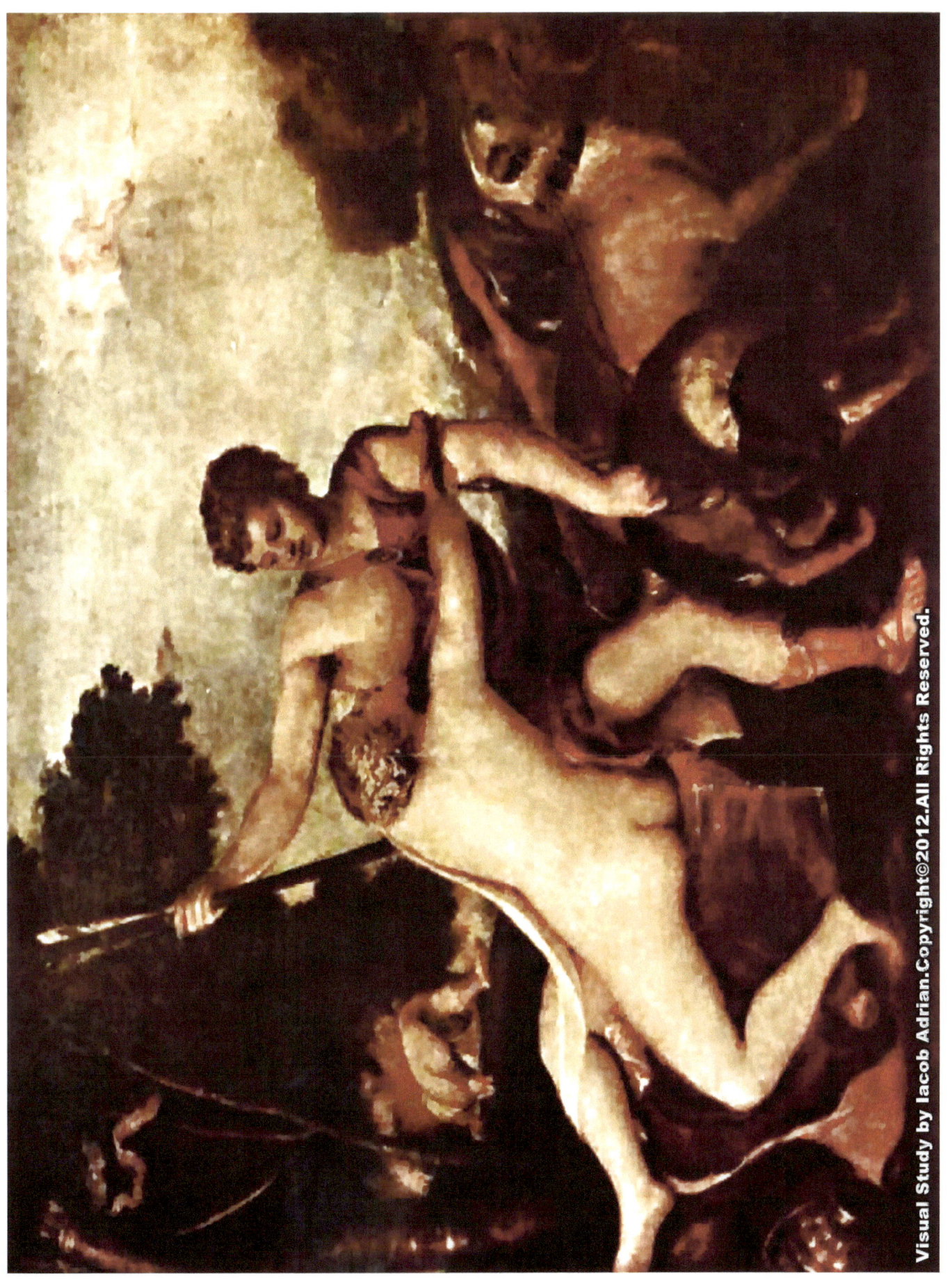

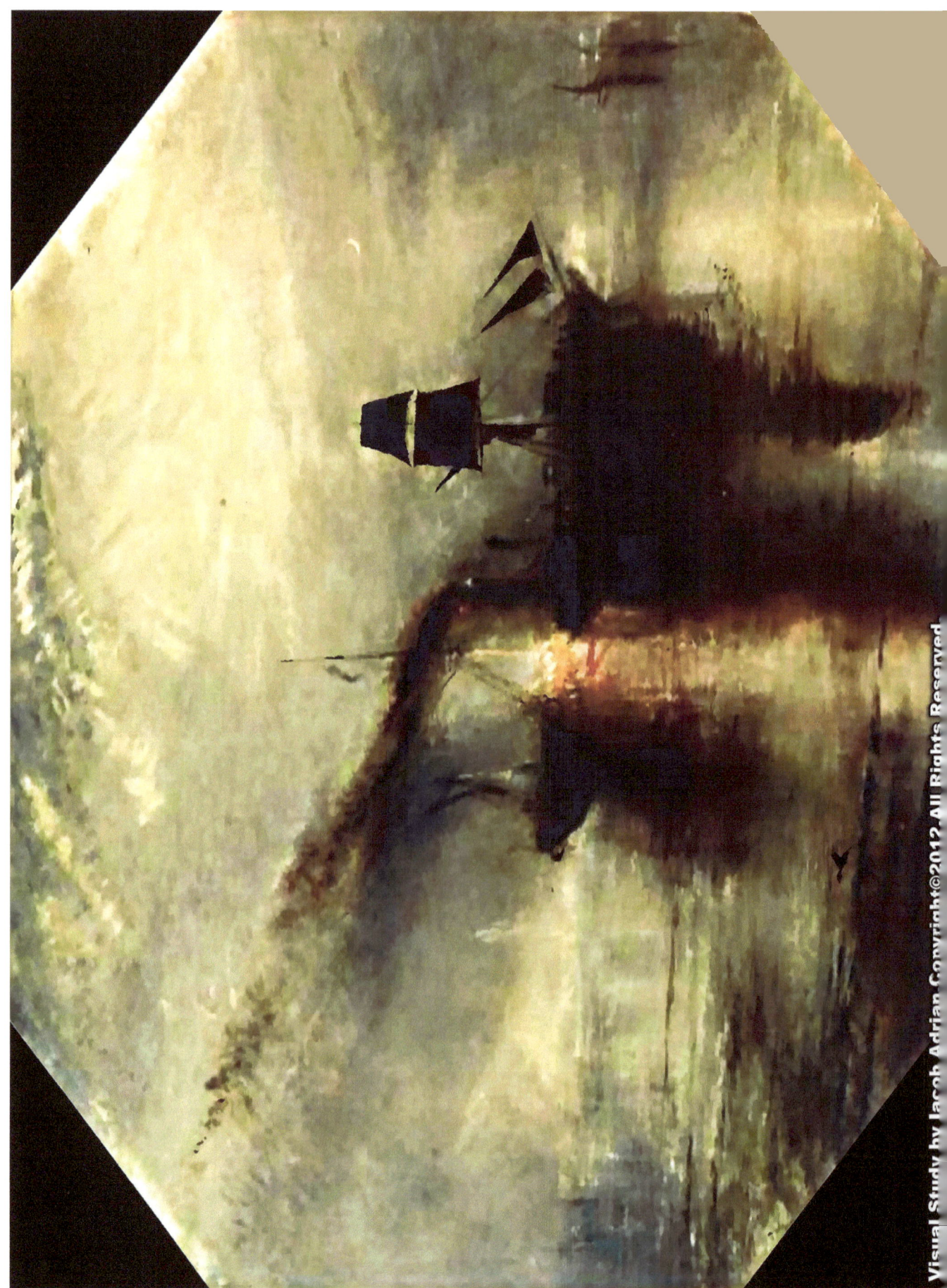

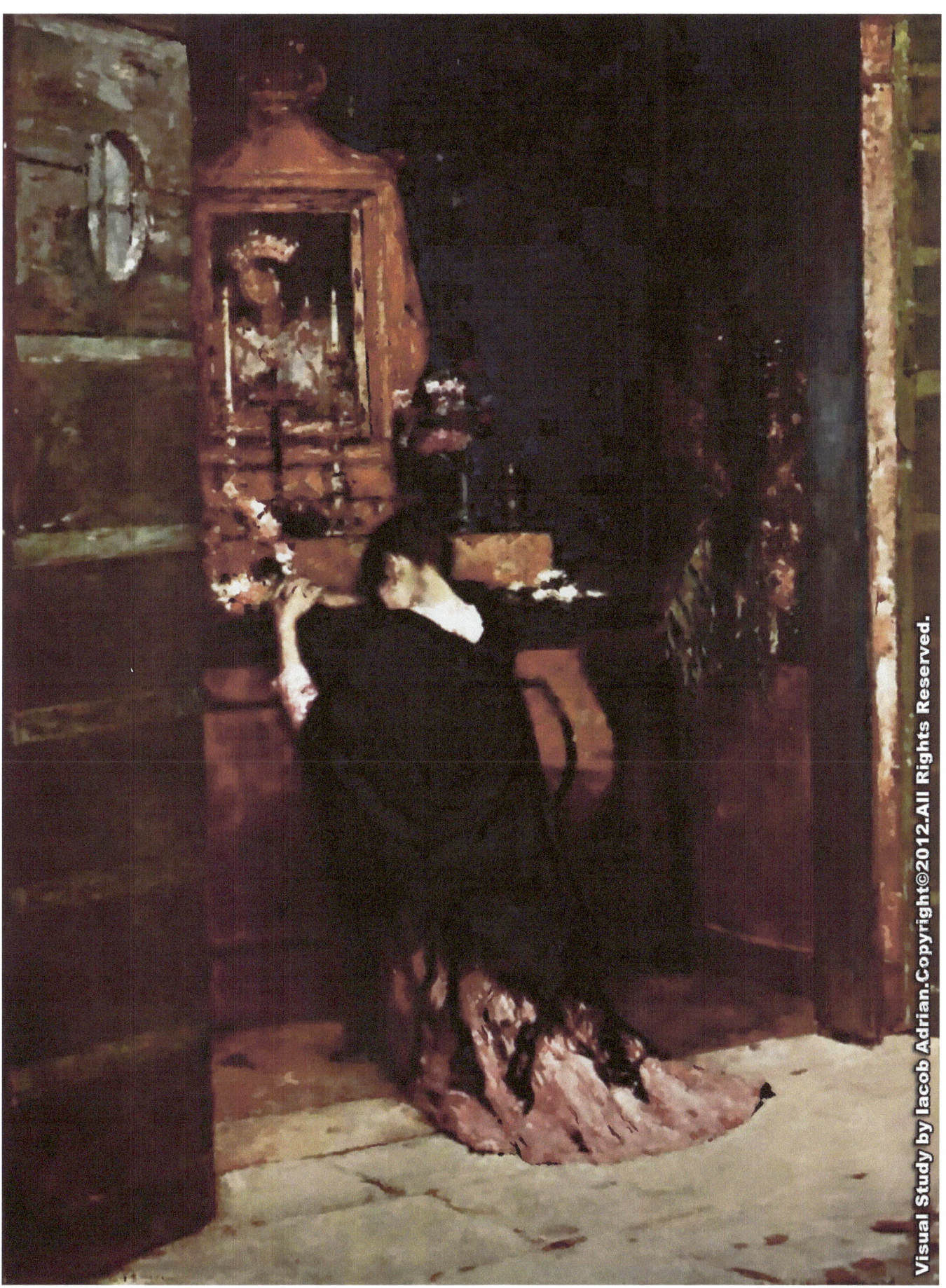

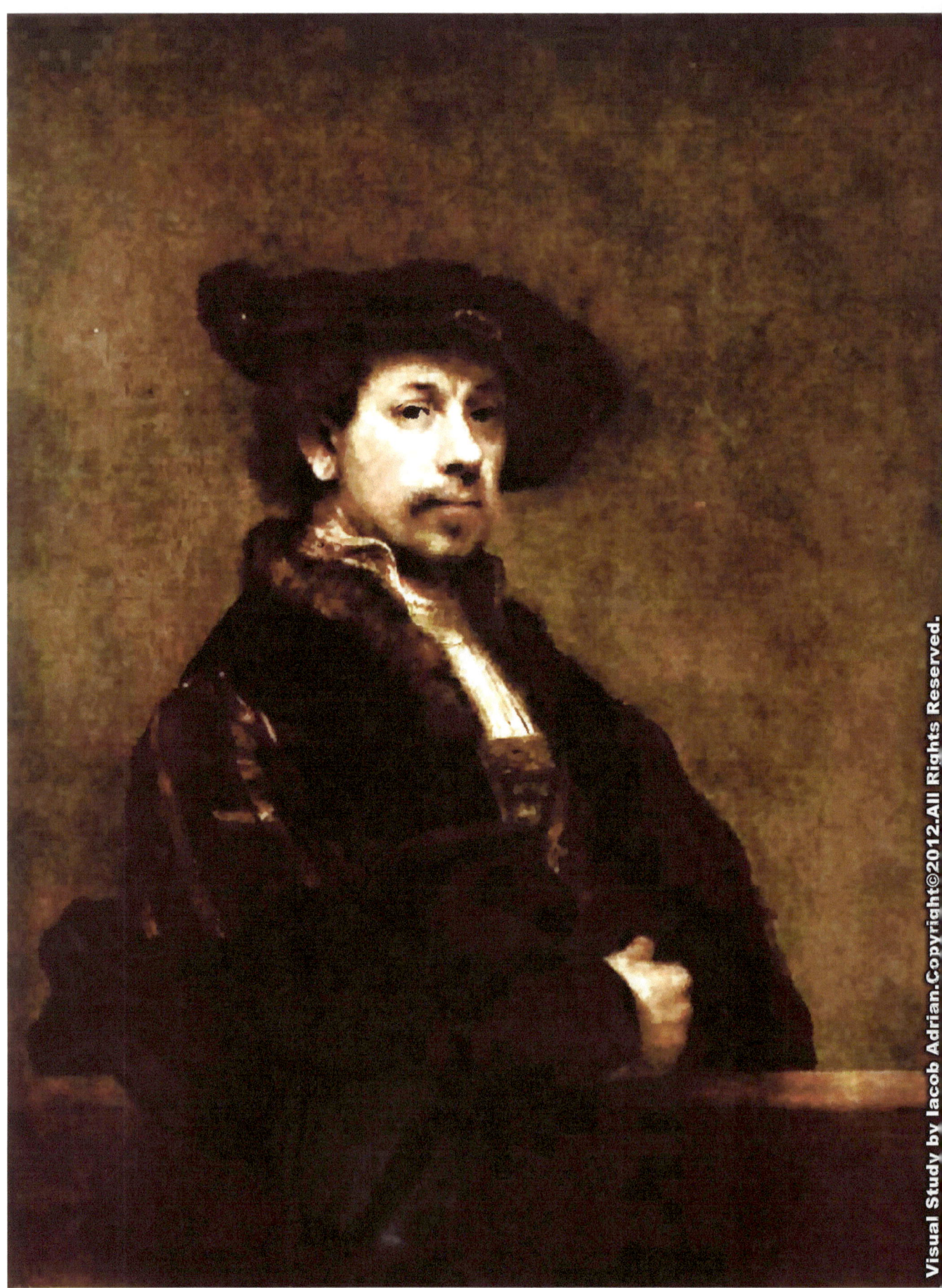

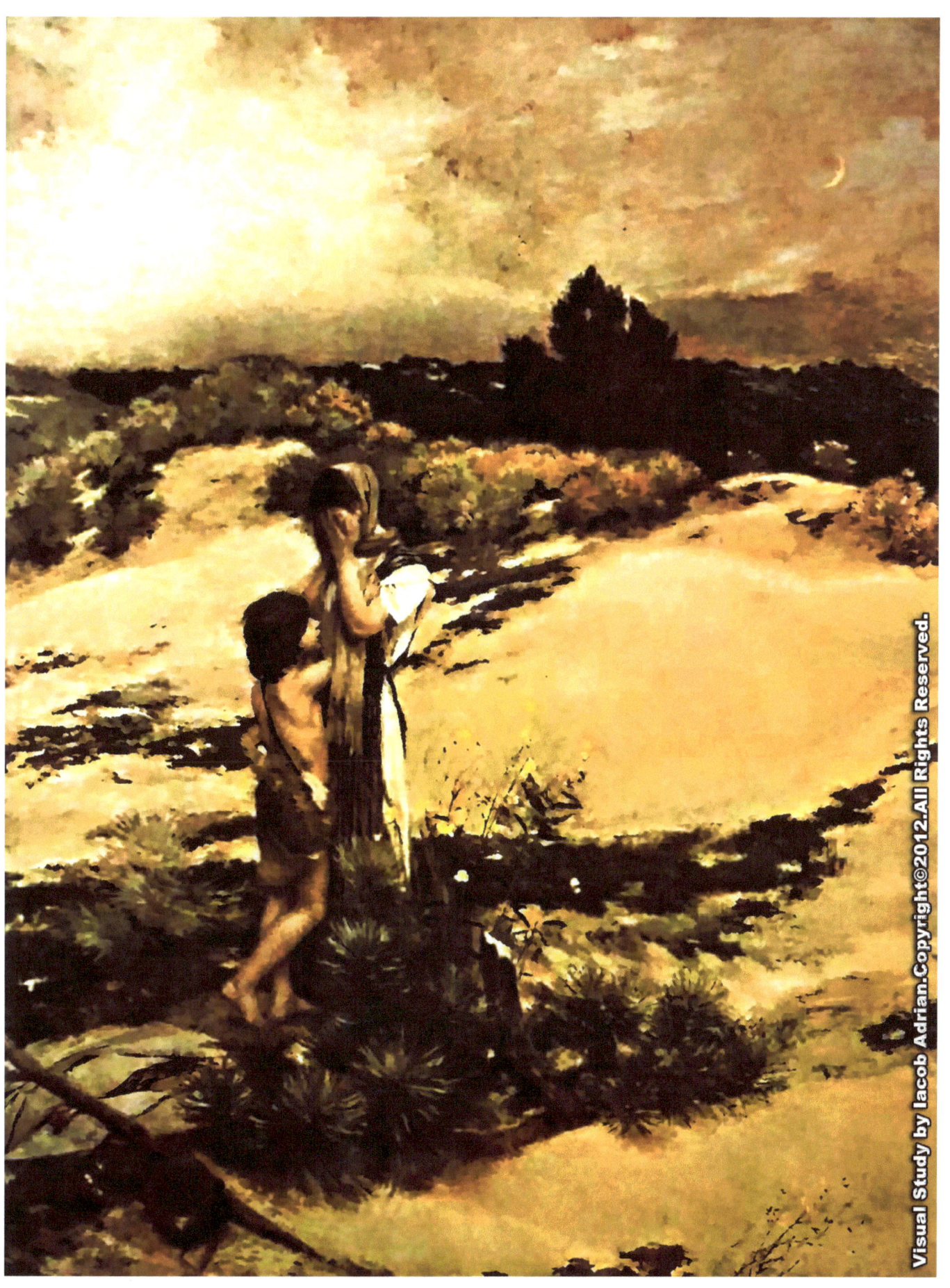

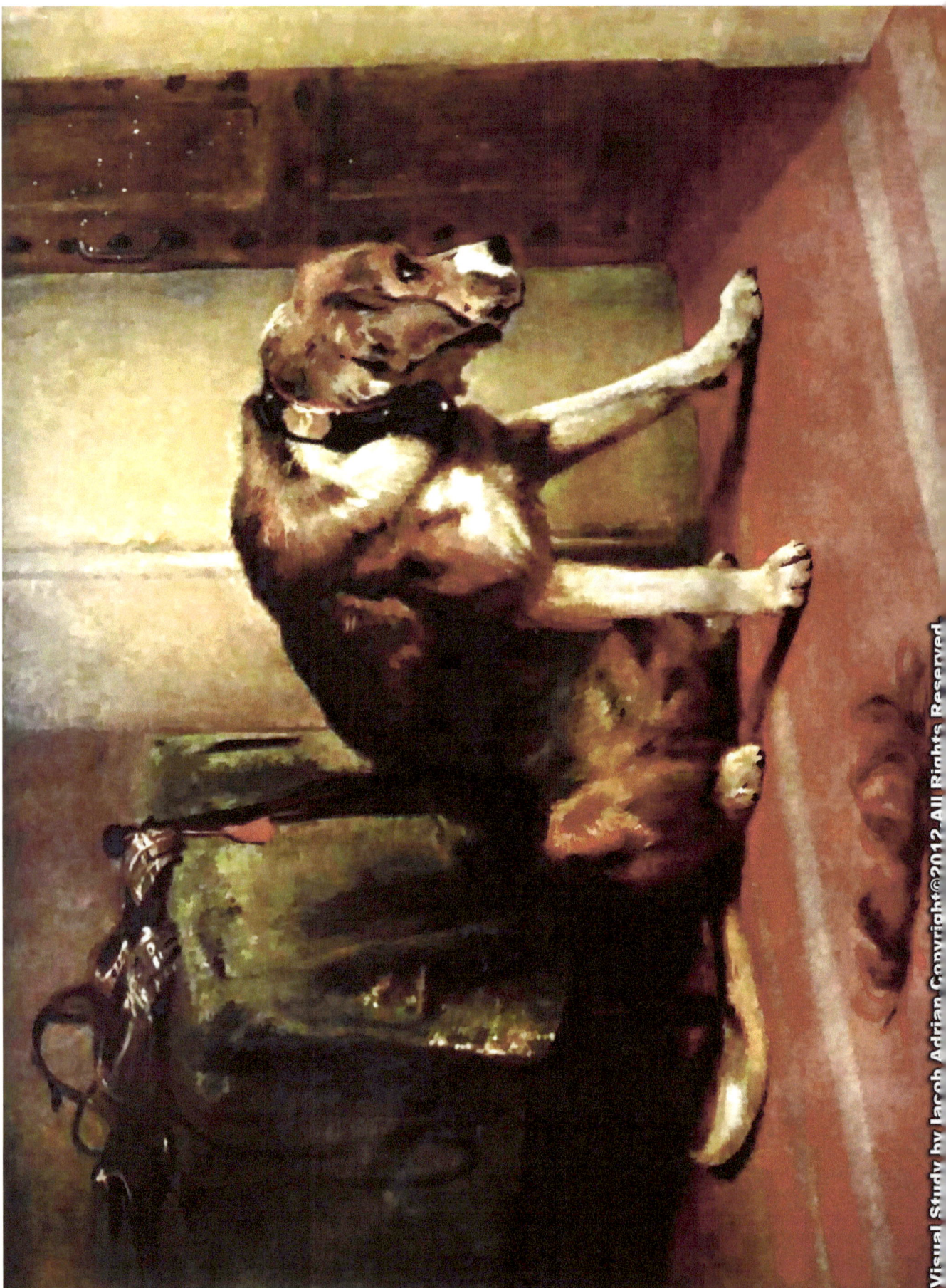

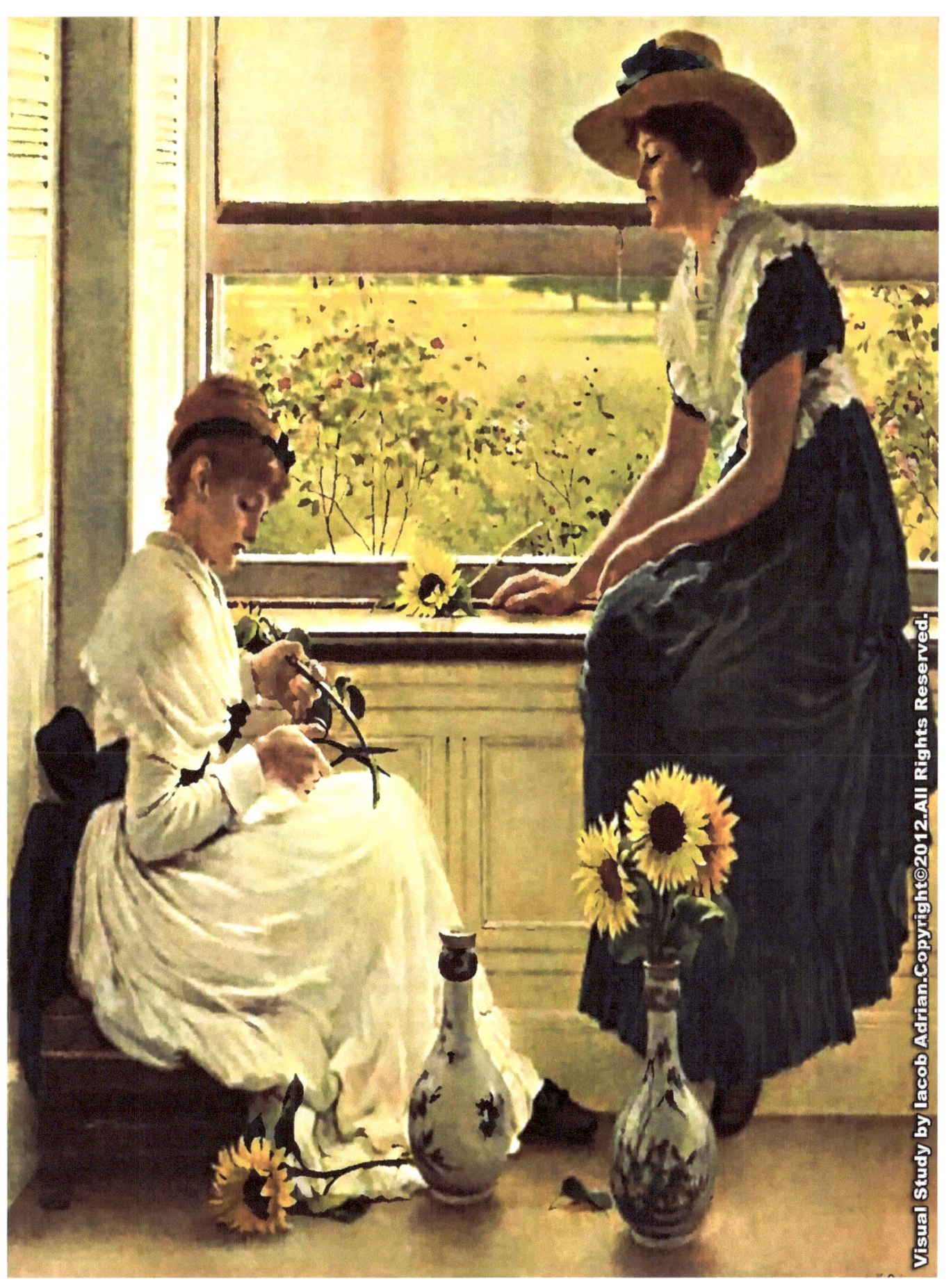

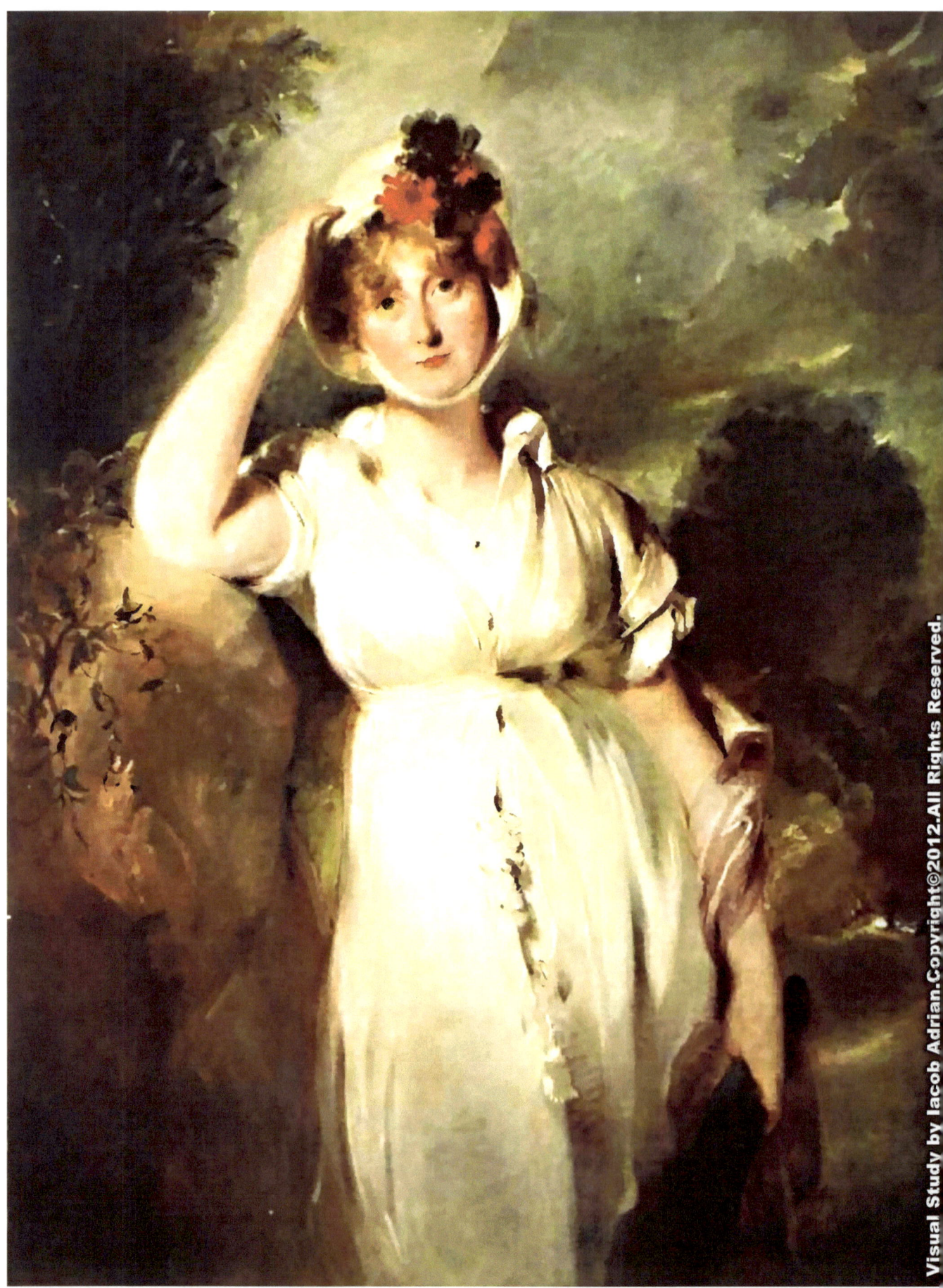

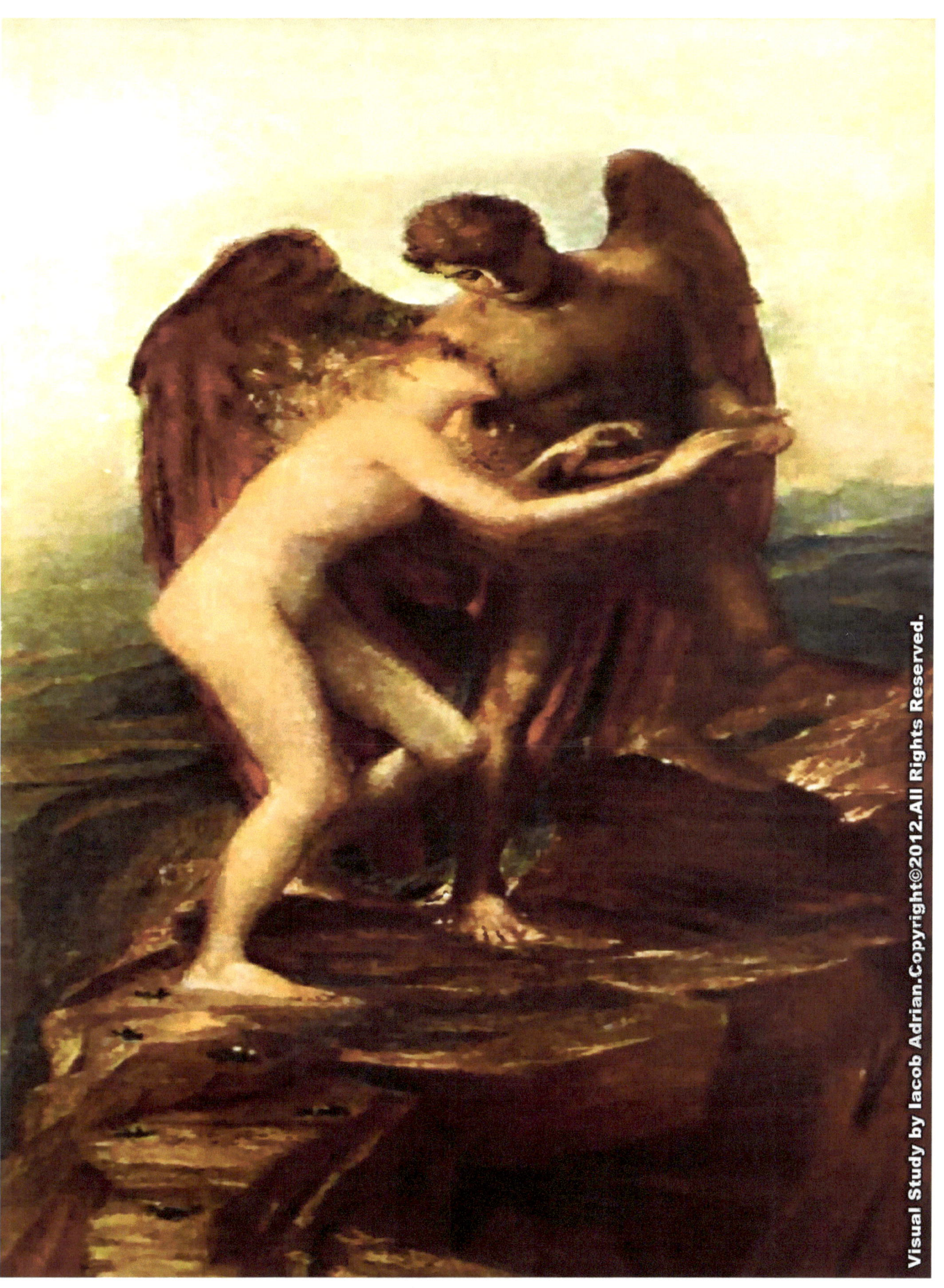

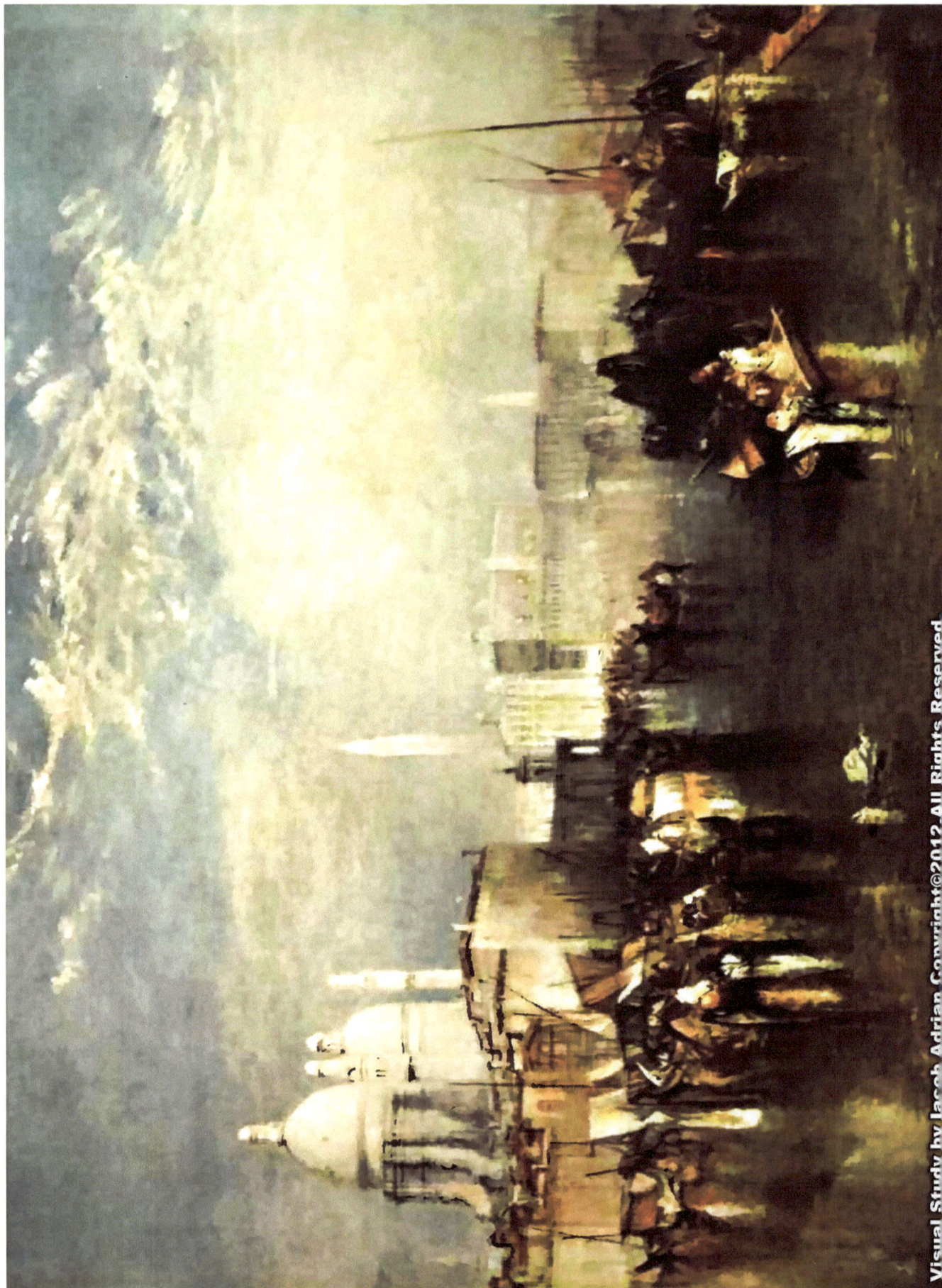

Bibliographic sources :

Famous Paintings selected from the world's great galleries and reproduced in colour (1913)

Author: Chesterton, G. K. (Gilbert Keith), 1874-1936. Introduction

Publisher: London ; New York ; Toronto : Cassell

This documentary study use, combined in various proportions, elements from the following categories, forms and subsets :
- fair use
- documentary
- documentary photography
- feature
- journalism
- arts journalism
- visual journalism
- photojournalism
- celebrity photography
in order to :
- employ material as the object of cultural critique ,
- quote to illustrate an argument or point ,
- use material in historical sequence,
providing independent opinion,
using photos, press articles, advertisements,
opinions of fans etc. ...

www.ingramcontent.com/pod-product-compliance
Lightning Source LLC
Chambersburg PA
CBHW041300180526
45172CB00003B/910